EGYPTIAN DELTA ARCHAEOLOGY

sidestone press

Willem van Haarlem

EGYPTIAN DELTA ARCHAEOLOGY

Short studies in honour of Willem van Haarlem

edited by
Ben van den Bercken

Published by Sidestone Press, Leiden
www.sidestone.com

In collaboration with Allard Pierson – the collections of the University of Amsterdam
www.allardpierson.nl

ALLARDPIERSON
THE COLLECTIONS OF THE UNIVERSITY OF AMSTERDAM

Lay-out & cover design: Sidestone Press

Photograph cover: shabti of the priest Hor, faience, h. 20 cm, 26th dynasty, image Allard Pierson, University of Amsterdam, APM08854; Egyptian Delta landscape, image AdobeStock; Willem van Haarlem at Tell Ibrahim Awad in 2012, image Ron Leenheer; statuette of a cat, bronze, h. 17.5 cm, 26th dynasty, image Allard Pierson, University of Amsterdam, APM08831

Photograph title page: Willem van Haarlem at Tell Ibrahim Awad in 2012, image Ron Leenheer

Copy editing: Noctua Text & Translation / Corinna Vermeulen
www.noctua-text-translation.eu

ISBN 978-94-6426-009-0 (softcover)
ISBN 978-94-6426-010-6 (hardcover)
ISBN 978-94-6426-011-3 (PDF e-book)

M
mondriaan
fund

This publication was realised with the support of the Mondriaan Fund, the public fund for visual art and cultural heritage

Contents

Preface and acknowledgements

Wim Hupperetz and Ben van den Bercken

The ancient-Egyptian collection of the Allard Pierson – the museum that holds the varied heritage collections of the University of Amsterdam – was presented in new galleries in the summer of 2020. This fresh display was part of the completely renewed collection presentation titled *From the Nile to the Amstel*, which emphasises the relations between the different cultures of the ancient world and beyond. During the preparations for the new galleries the two curators of the Egyptian collection, Willem van Haarlem and Ben van den Bercken, regularly discussed the project, the collection, its history and anecdotes over a cup of coffee. The new presentation is one of the last projects of the senior curator, Willem van Haarlem. During these pleasant coffee sessions the idea arose to organise a publication dedicated to Willem on the occasion of his retirement at the Allard Pierson. The idea took further shape and despite the limited amount of time available it was decided that this project should be started as soon as possible and realised at the date of Willem's retirement after forty years at the Allard Pierson.

Although generally speaking it is good for people to change jobs after a few years, museum curators tend to hold the same position for up to a lifetime. Not only is it a reward and honour for the passionate curator to be able to work with highly interesting artefacts within one particular field of study, this concentration on one collection also deepens his or her knowledge of it. One of the first of Willem's projects at the Allard Pierson (Museum) was meant to chart and extend the existing knowledge of the Egyptian collection. This resulted in a thorough study on the ancient Egyptian objects of the Allard Pierson in four volumes of the international loose-leaf catalogue series Corpus Antiquitatum Aegyptiacarum (CAA). Preparations for an Amsterdam volume in this series had already been started in 1975, when the idea was launched by Joris F. Borghouts (1939-2018). He had been appointed lecturer at the Egyptological Institute of the University of Amsterdam in 1969.[1] Willem obtained his degree in Egyptology at the University of Amsterdam in 1981 and started working as an editor on the first CAA volume in that same year. It was a cross-section of the collection containing entries about several of the most important

1 Kaper 2014, 51.

in: Bercken, B.J.L. van den, 2021. *Egyptian Delta archaeology. Short studies in honour of Willem van Haarlem*, Leiden: Sidestone Press, pp. 7-12.

Fig. 1 Shabtis from the New Kingdom to the Late Period in the renewed Egyptian room *Journey through the Underworld* (2020).

objects.[2] Together with his former fellow student Mario J. de Bruyn, Willem wrote most of the entries for the first volume, to which five entries by Robert Lunsingh Scheurleer and Els de Heer-Scholtens were added. Three more volumes for the Amsterdam CAA followed between 1990 and 1998.[3] The second volume, on the shabtis, mirrored Willem's lifetime interest in shabtis which was already visible in early contributions to the bulletin for the friends of the museum and can be seen in the new galleries as well (fig. 1).[4] Over the years, this pillar of the Egyptian collection in Amsterdam has enabled numerous studies and exhibitions at the Allard Pierson on topics related to ancient Egypt.

Two years before obtaining his degree, Willem joined the archaeological excavation at Tell ed-Dab'a directed by Manfred Bietak. The archaeological importance of the Nile Delta was already being emphasised at that time and the urgency of documenting sites has been increasing ever since. Together with fellow students, Willem was introduced to the life of an archaeologist in Egypt and he liked it. In fact, he never let it go for the rest of his career. New discoveries at the site fed his interest in ancient Egypt and in 1982 he also joined the team working at Qantir/Piramesse directed by Edgar B. Pusch. Inspired by his love for fieldwork, Willem continued to work alternately for both projects for over a decade. With this fieldwork experience he was appointed field director of the excavation by the Nederlandse Stichting voor Archeologisch Onderzoek in Egypte (Netherlands Foundation for Archaeological Research in Egypt) at Tell Ibrahim Awad in 1991. This promising site

2 Van Haarlem 1986.

3 Van Haarlem 1990; Van Haarlem 1995; and Van Haarlem 1998.

4 Van Haarlem 1978, 3-4; Van Haarlem 1985, 14-15.

Fig. 2 Willem photographing at site A at Tell Ibrahim Awad in 1993 (image Ron Leenheer).

had been mapped by the Amsterdam University survey expedition in the previous years.[5] Together with Tell el-Iswid, Tell Ibrahim Awad had been chosen for a test trench excavation and subsequently a more extensive excavation was started at Tell Ibrahim Awad.

Over the following years, the project focused on two locations there: 1) site B, which yielded a number of early dynastic tombs and an early dynastic settlement;[6] and 2) site A, where the stratigraphy indicated a number of phases involving temple building and use on the same location from *c.*3300 to 1950 BC as well as remains of a settlement (fig. 2). Willem continued working at the site with an international team until 2014 (fig. 3). From 1999 to 2003 he combined his fieldwork and work at the Allard Pierson with a position as assistant director at the Dutch-Flemish Institute in Cairo. Organising the annual 'Cairo semester' is an important part of this job. As part of the graduate school programme, it introduces students of Egyptology and archaeology to ancient as well as modern Egypt. In 2016 and 2017 Willem and Wim Hupperetz visited Luxor and Edfu and participated in the excavation at Hierakonpolis.

---

5 Van Haarlem 2019, 9.

6 Van Haarlem 2019, 18.

Fig. 3 Willem inspecting the site at Tell Ibrahim Awad in 2012 (image Ron Leenheer).

From 2009 onwards the emphasis was more on the preparation of exhibitions, research projects and work on his dissertation, which he completed in 2014. In the exhibitions *The Judgement of the Dead* (2010), *Access Denied. Secrets of Egyptian Temples* (2011), *Eternal Egypt Experience* (2013-2014) and *Encounters with the Orient* (2016) the collection from pharaonic Egypt took centre stage. These exhibitions were in fact preparations for the renewal of the museum galleries within the new concept *From the Nile to the Amstel*. The projects *The Petrie Perspective* and *The Bissing Link* enabled the Allard Pierson to better document and trace the historiography of a part of its Egyptian collection. The biography of this and any other collection can only be understood through historical research on the networks of collectors throughout Europe and beyond. The dispersed collection of Friedrich Wilhelm Freiherr von Bissing (1873-1956) is the best example to lay bare these connections. Here we can discover important influences and scholarly agendas that explain the way these collections grew and eventually dispersed.

The contributions in this volume meet in one of Willem's favourite fields of study and the region where he first excavated in Egypt: the Nile Delta. As the curator regularly is a bridge between archaeological fieldwork and the work in the museum, Willem's colleagues from both fields have contributed to this volume. Thanks are first and foremost due to these authors, with whom Willem worked over the years. They found the time and resources during the Covid-19 pandemic to write an attractive variety of short contributions. We are grateful to the colleagues at the Allard Pierson and the Egyptological community for

Fig. 4 Willem (in front of left column) during the annual CIPEG General Assembly at the Glyptotek in Copenhagen in 2014 (image CIPEG).

providing details and image material (fig. 4).[7] This publication was coordinated by junior curator Ben van den Bercken and realised by the Allard Pierson's publications manager, Paulien Retèl. Special thanks are due to the publisher, Sidestone Press, who made this volume possible in a relatively short period.

It is with the greatest pleasure that the Allard Pierson offers Willem this publication in his honour. We wish him a happy retirement and good luck with all his future projects, which will undoubtedly involve ancient Egypt.

Bibliography

Haarlem, W. van, 1978, Sjawabti's uit de collectie Dobber, *Mededelingenblad. Vereniging van Vrienden Allard Pierson Museum* 15, Amsterdam, 3-4.

Haarlem, W. van, 1985, Een koninklijke familie in het museum, *Mededelingenblad. Vereniging van Vrienden Allard Pierson Museum* 35, Amsterdam, 14-15.

Haarlem, W. van (ed.), 1986, Allard Pierson Museum, Amsterdam, fascicle 1: selection from the collection, *Corpus antiquitatum Aegyptiacarum*, Amsterdam.

Haarlem, W. van (ed.), 1990, Allard Pierson Museum, Amsterdam, fascicle 2: shabtis, *Corpus antiquitatum Aegyptiacarum*, Amsterdam.

Haarlem, W. van (ed.), 1995, Allard Pierson Museum, Amsterdam, fascicle 3: stelae and reliefs, *Corpus antiquitatum Aegyptiacarum*, Amsterdam.

---

7 In this regard we would like to thank Tine Bagh, Rob Demarée, Jacobus van Dijk, Jorrit Kelder, Ron Leenheer and Marleen De Meyer.

Haarlem, W. van (ed.), 1998, Allard Pierson Museum, Amsterdam, fascicle 4: sarcophagi and related objects, *Corpus antiquitatum Aegyptiacarum*, Amsterdam.

Haarlem, W. van, 2019, *Temple deposits in Early Dynastic Egypt: the case of Tell Ibrahim Awad. BAR International Series* 2931, Oxford.

Kaper, O.E., 2014, De geschiedenis van de egyptologie aan Nederlandse universiteiten, in Kaper, O.E., Dercksen, J.G. (eds.), 2014, *Waar de geschiedenis begon. Nederlandse onderzoekers in de ban van spijkerschrift, hiërogliefen en aardewerk*, Leuven, 39-61.

About the authors

Wim Hupperetz, director of the Allard Pierson, is a heritage specialist in the field of museology, design, cultural landscape and urban environment; he focuses on creating additional value by interactive and virtual media and a multidisciplinary approach. Specialises in work related to museology, archaeology, town planning and historical research aimed at heritage issues. Concept developer/initiator of the Heritage Lab (2011), New Media/Digital Museum Lab (2012), ArcheoHotspots (2014), museum network COBBRA (2015), CEMEC EU project (2015), Collectors Cabinet (2016), MuseumCamp (2016), Cross Culture Timeline (2017) and Allard Pierson Live (2018), which led to the renewal of the Allard Pierson in 2020.

Ben van den Bercken is an archaeologist and junior curator of Egyptian antiquities at the Allard Pierson, University of Amsterdam. Formerly, he was assistant curator of Engraved Gems at the National Museum of Antiquities, Leiden. His work on the Leiden collection of engraved gems includes contributions to the collection's history and studies of Egyptian scarabs and Egyptian cylinder seals. He worked at excavations in Alexandria, Egypt. Presently, he is working on the history of the Egyptian collection of the Allard Pierson and a project on mummy portraits.

Bibliography Willem van Haarlem[1]

2020

Haarlem, W. van, 2020, De mummie van een krokodil, *Allard Pierson Mededelingen* 122, 27.

Haarlem, W. van, Beek, R. van, Jurriaans-Helle, G., 2020, Geschenken van een bijzondere vriendin. De archeologische collectie van Marion Mosler, *Allard Pierson Mededelingen* 121, 21-25.

2019

Haarlem, W. van, 2019, Monumentale biografie uit het elitegraf van Mehi, *Allard Pierson Mededelingen* 120, 14-15.

Haarlem, W. van, 2019, Een loflied op de zon bij de ingang van een graf, *Allard Pierson Mededelingen* 120, 12-13.

Haarlem, W. van, 2019, Ontstaan van schrift, staat en koningschap, 3300-100 v.Chr, *Allard Pierson Mededelingen* 120, 11.

Haarlem, W. van, 2019, *Temple deposits in Early Dynastic Egypt: the case of Tell Ibrahim Awad. BAR International Series* 2931, Oxford.

Haarlem, W. van, 2019, "But he has broken every jar in the place, as he said he would.": letters of Petrie to von Bissing: a short contribution to the history of Egyptology, *Journal of Egyptian Archaeology* 105 (1), 143-147.

2018

Haarlem, W. van, 2018, De Egyptische make-up paletten in het museum, *Allard Pierson Mededelingen* 117, 2-7.

1 This bibliography does not include contributions of Willem van Haarlem to exhibition catalogues, e.g. Quertinmont, A. (ed.), 2016, *Dieux, genies et demons en Égypte ancienne: à la recontre d'Osiris, Anubis, Isis, Hathor, Rê et les autres: catalogue d'exposition, Musée Royal de Mariemont*, Paris and Rammant-Peeters, A. (ed.), 1994, *Palmen en tempels: Fotografie in Egypte in de XIXe eeuw*, Leuven; or short archaeological reports e.g. Institut Français d'Archéologie Orientale 1998. Bulletin d'information archéologique 9-10 (1994). Le Caire. Any omissions or mistakes in the list are the responsibility of the editor.

in: Bercken, B.J.L. van den, 2021. *Egyptian Delta archaeology. Short studies in honour of Willem van Haarlem*, Leiden: Sidestone Press, pp. 13-20.

Haarlem, W. van, 2018, Review of: Kahl, J., Deppe, N., Goldsmith, D., Kilian, A., Kitagawa, C., Moje, J., Zöller-Engelhardt, M., 2016, Asyut, Tomb III: objects (part 1). The Asyut Project 3. Wiesbaden, *Bibliotheca Orientalis* 75 (1-2), 92-93.

2017

Haarlem, W. van, 2017, Nieuwe leden van de koninklijke familie, *Allard Pierson Mededelingen* 116, 2-4.

Haarlem, W. van, 2017, The papyrus puzzle, or how to unlock a random papyrus collection? in Derriks, C. (ed.), 2017, *Collections at risk: new challenges in a new environment. Proceedings of the 29th CIPEG Annual Meeting in Brussels, September 25-28, 2012, Royal Museum of Art and History, Brussels, Belgium*, Atlanta, 117-120.

2016

Haarlem, W. van, 2016, Twee reliëfs herenigd, *Allard Pierson Mededelingen* 111/112, 28-29.

Haarlem, W. van, 2016, Petrie en het Allard Pierson, *Allard Pierson Mededelingen* 111/112, 9-15.

Haarlem, W. van, 2016, Review of: Janßen, U., 2015, Gesellschaften im Wandel: funerärer Aufwand und soziale Wirklichkeit im frühstaatlichen Mesopotamien und Ägypten anhand von Grabbefunden aus Ur und Kafr Tarkhan. Schriften zur Vorderasiatischen Archäologie 10, Wiesbaden, *Bibliotheca Orientalis* 73 (5-6), 791-793.

2015

Haarlem, W. van, 2015, In Memoriam. Prof. Dr. M.S.H.G. Heerma van Voss (Matthieu) 1923-2015, *Allard Pierson Mededelingen* 110, 33.

2014

Haarlem, W. van, 2014, Lotgevallen van een verzamelaar: Friedrich Wilhelm von Bissing (1873-1956), *Allard Pierson Mededelingen* 109, 2-5.

Haarlem, W. van, 2014, Temple deposits in Early Dynastic Egypt: the case of Tell Ibrahim Awad (dissertation).

Haarlem, W. van, 2014, Review of: Moje, J., 2013, The ushebtis from early excavations in the necropolis of Asyut, mainly by David George Hogarth and Ahmed Bey Kamal: with remarks on ushebti iconography and related burial practices in Asyut from the New Kingdom to the Ptolemaic period. The Asyut Project 4, Wiesbaden, *Chronique d'Égypte* 89 (177), 90-91.

2013

Haarlem, W. van, 2013, Review of: Bußmann, R., 2010, Die Provinztempel Ägyptens von der 0. bis zur 11. Dynastie: Archäologie und Geschichte einer gesellschaftlichen Institution zwischen Residenz und Provinz, Probleme der Ägyptologie 30, Leiden, *Orientalistische Literaturzeitung* 108 (1), 11-12.

Haarlem, W. van, Bercken, B. van den (eds.), 2013, Eternal Egypt, Zwolle.

Haarlem, W. van, Bercken, B. van den (eds.), 2013, Eeuwig Egypte, Zwolle.

2012

Haarlem, W. van, 2012, Some uncommon pottery from Tell Ibrahim Awad (Eastern Delta), *Göttinger Miszellen* 233, 91-93.

2011

Haarlem, W. van, 2011, Talloos veel goden, *Allard Pierson Mededelingen* 104, 8-15.

Haarlem, W. van, 2011, Huizen van Miljoenen Jaren, *Allard Pierson Mededelingen* 104, 2-7.

Haarlem, W. van, 2011, De (Nederlandse) opgravingen op Tell Ibrahim Awad in de Nijldelta, *Ta-Mery* 4, 104-111.

2010

Haarlem, W. van, 2010, Het graf van Alexander de Grote, *Allard Pierson Mededelingen* 103, 21.

Haarlem, W. van, Wiegers, G., 2010, Dies Irae. Het oordeel over de doden en het Paradijs in het Christendom en de Islam, *Allard Pierson Mededelingen* 101, 28-32.

Haarlem, W. van, 2010, Het Egyptische Dodenboek, *Allard Pierson Mededelingen* 101, 13-15.

Haarlem, W. van, 2010, De sarcofaag van Teuris, *Allard Pierson Mededelingen* 101, 8-11.

Haarlem, W. van, 2010, Het Egyptische dodengericht, *Allard Pierson Mededelingen* 101, 2-7.

Haarlem, W. van, 2010, Firepots in firepits: an enigma, *Göttinger Miszellen* 224, 101-104.

2009

Haarlem, W. van, 2009, Eindelijk weer zijn identiteit terug, *Allard Pierson Mededelingen* 100, 14-15.

Haarlem, W. van, 2009, Een beschimmeld geschenk, *Mededelingenblad. Vereniging van Vrienden Allard Pierson Museum* 98/99, 4-6.

Phillips, D.L., Rose, J.C., Haarlem, W. van, 2009, Bioarchaeology of Tell Ibrahim Awad, *Ägypten und Levante* 19, 157-210.

Haarlem, W. van, 2009, Temple deposits at Tell Ibrahim Awad, Amsterdam.

Haarlem, W. van, 2009, Review of: Bonnet, C., Valbelle, D., 2006, Pharaonen aus dem schwarzen Afrika, *PalArch's Journal of Archaeology of Egypt/Egyptology* 6(3), 2-3.

Haarlem, W. van, 2009, Review of: Bard, K.A., 2008, An introduction to the archaeology of ancient Egypt, *PalArch's Journal of Archaeology of Egypt/Egyptology* 6(3), 1-2.

2008

Haarlem, W. van, Berg, J. van den, 2008, Een Thebaanse sarcofaag in het museum, *Mededelingenblad. Vereniging van Vrienden Allard Pierson Museum* 97, 6-11.

Van Haarlem, W. van, 2008, Review of: Jánosi, P., 2006, Die Gräberwelt der Pyramidenzeit, *PalArch's Journal of Archaeology of Egypt/Egyptology* 6.

2007

Haarlem, W. van, 2007, Bronzen votiefbeelden uit Egypte, *Mededelingenblad. Vereniging van Vrienden Allard Pierson Museum* 95, 15-19.

Haarlem, W. van, 2007, Een 'koninklijke' baksteen uit Egypte, *Mededelingenblad. Vereniging van Vrienden Allard Pierson Museum* 94, 4-5.

2006

Haarlem, W. van, 2006, Een zeldzame lijkkist uit Egypte, *Mededelingenblad. Vereniging van Vrienden Allard Pierson Museum* 93, 4-9.

Haarlem, W. van, 2006, Watermanagement in de oudheid, *Mededelingenblad. Vereniging van Vrienden Allard Pierson Museum* 91/92, 26-27.

Haarlem, W. van, Hikade, T., 2006, Recent results of research at Tell Ibrahim Awad, in Czerny, E., Hein, I., Hunger, H., Melman, D., Schwab, A. (eds.), *Timelines: studies in honour of Manfred Bietak 1*, Leuven, 389-398.

2005

Haarlem, W. van, 2005, The First Intermediate Period cemetery and settlement at Tell Ibrahim Awad, in Pantalacci, L., Berger-El-Naggar, C. (eds.), *Des Néferkarê aux Montouhotep: travaux archéologiques en cours sur la fin de la VIe dynastie et la première période intermédiaire; actes du colloque CNRS-Université Lumière-Lyon 2, tenu le 5-7 juillet 2001, Lyon*, Paris, 195-202.

2004

Haarlem, W. van, 2004, Het prinsesje hersteld, *Mededelingenblad. Vereniging van Vrienden Allard Pierson Museum* 89, 4-5.

Haarlem, W. van, 2004, De farao hoeft zijn hoofd niet meer te breken, *Mededelingenblad. Vereniging van Vrienden Allard Pierson Museum* 89, 2-3.

Haarlem, W. van, 2004, Catalogisering van de Egyptische voorwerpen in het museum, *Mededelingenblad. Vereniging van Vrienden Allard Pierson Museum* 88, 18-19.

2003

Haarlem, W. van, 2003, The excavations at Tell Ibrahim Awad (Sharqiya Province), seasons 1995-2000, in Hawass, Z., Pinch Brock, L. (eds.), 2003, *Egyptology at the dawn of the twenty-first century: proceedings of the Eighth International Congress of Egyptologists, Cairo, 2000 1*, Cairo, 536-540.

Haarlem, W. van, 2003, *Graven in de Nijldelta. Ervaringen van een Nederlandse archeoloog in Egypte*, Baarn.

2002

Haarlem, W. van, 2002, History of the excavations at Tell Ibrahim Awad (Eastern Nile Delta) / История раскопок в Телль Ибрагим Аваде (Восточная Дельта Нила), in Belova, G.A., Sherkova, T.A., 2002, *Ancient Egyptian temple at Tell Ibrahim Awad: excavations and discoveries in the Nile Delta / Древнеегипетский храм в Телль Ибрагим Аваде: раскопки и открытия в Дельте Нила*, Moscow, 16-22, 106-111.

Rose, J.C., Haarlem, W. van, 2002, The people of Tell Ibrahim Awad in the Nile Delta / Население Телль Ибрагим Авада в Дельте Нила, in Belova, G.A., Sherkova, T.A., 2002, *Ancient Egyptian temple at Tell Ibrahim Awad: excavations and discoveries in the Nile Delta / Древнеегипетский храм в Телль Ибрагим Аваде: раскопки и открытия в Дельте Нила*, Moscow, 42-51, 130-137.

Haarlem, W. van, 2002, The ivory objects from Tell Ibrahim Awad, *Egyptian Archaeology* 20, 16-17.

2001

Haarlem, W. van, 2001, Tell Ibrahim Awad. *Egyptian Archaeology* 18, 33-35.

Rose, J.C., Haarlem, W. van, 2001, First Intermediate Period mortuary patterns at Tell Ibrahim Awad in the eastern Nile Delta, in Sherkova, T.A. (ed.), *История и культура древнего и раннехристианского Египта: материалы научной конференции, посвященной 100-летию со дня рождения М.Э. Матье и М.А. Коростовцева. 13-15 декебра 2000 г.*, Moscow, 141-148.

2000

Haarlem, W. van, 2000, Apen in de Delta, *Mededelingenblad. Vereniging van Vrienden Allard Pierson Museum* 78, 14-17.

Haarlem, W. van, 2000, Het Oudegyptische schriftsysteem, *Mededelingenblad. Vereniging van Vrienden Allard Pierson Museum* 77, 6-9.

Haarlem, W. van, 2000, Review of: Wilkinson, T.A.H., 1999, Early dynastic Egypt. London, *Journal of Egyptian Archaeology* 86, 188-189.

Haarlem, W. van, 2000, An introduction to the site of Tell Ibrahim Awad, *Ägypten und Levante* 10, 13-16.

Haarlem, W. van, 2000, Mummification and religion, *Talanta* 30-31, 191-193.

Haarlem, W. van, 2000, De opgravingen te Tell Ibrahim Awad, 1994-2000, *Phoenix* 46, 128-135.

1999

Haarlem, W. van, 1999, A predynastic triple vessel from Tell Ibrahim Awad, *Göttinger Miszellen* 173, 193-197.

1998

Haarlem, W. van, Jurriaans-Helle, G., 1998, Catalogus, *Mededelingenblad. Vereniging van Vrienden Allard Pierson Museum* 72/73, 35-39.

Haarlem, W. van, 1998, Geschiedenis en religie van de Kopten, *Mededelingenblad. Vereniging van Vrienden Allard Pierson Museum* 72/73, 2-4.

Haarlem, W. van, 1998, Mummy portraits: a review of some recent publications, *Göttinger Miszellen* 167, 109-112.

Haarlem, W. van, 1998, The excavations at Tell Ibrahim Awad (Eastern Nile Delta): recent results, in Eyre, C. J. (ed.), *Proceedings of the Seventh International Congress of Egyptologists, Cambridge, 3-9 September 1995*, Leuven, 509-513.

Haarlem, W. van, 1998, Les fouilles à Tell Ibrahim Awad (delta oriental du Nil): résultats récents, *Bulletin de la Société Française d'Égyptologie* 141, 8-19.

Haarlem, W. van, 1998, Allard Pierson Museum, Amsterdam, fascicle 4: sarcophagi and related objects. Corpus antiquitatum Aegyptiacarum: Lose-Blatt-Katalog ägyptischer Altertümer. Amsterdam: Allard Pierson Museum.

Haarlem, W. van, 1998, Archaic shrine models from Tell Ibrahim Awad, *Mitteilungen des Deutschen Archäologischen Instituts, Abteilung Kairo* 54, 183-185.

Rose, J.C., Benoit, P.H., Tucker, T.L., Haarlem, W. van, 1998, Tell Ibrahim Awad: bioarchaeology, dental microwear and postmortem chemical deposition, in Eyre, C.J. (ed.), 1998, *Proceedings of the Seventh International Congress of Egyptologists, Cambridge, 3-9 September 1995*, Leuven, 983-990.

Haarlem, W. van, 1998, Een geschenk voor de Egyptische afdeling, *Mededelingenblad. Vereniging van Vrienden Allard Pierson Museum* 71, 23.

1997

Haarlem, W. van, 1997, Review of: Anonymous (ed.), 1995, Egypte onomwonden: Egyptische oudheden van museum Vleeshuis. Antwerpen, Antwerpen, *Bibliotheca Orientalis* 54 (5-6), 676.

Haarlem, W. van, 1997, Coffins and naoi as votive objects in Tell Ibrahim Awad, in Dijk, J. van (ed.), 1997, *Essays on ancient Egypt in honour of Herman te Velde*, Groningen, 167-169.

Haarlem, W. van, 1997, Imitations in pottery of stone vessels in a protodynastic tomb from Tell Ibrahim Awad, *Archéo-Nil* 7, 145-150.

1996

Haarlem, W. van, 1996, Temple deposits at Tell Ibrahim Awad, II: an update, *Göttinger Miszellen* 154, 31-34.

Haarlem, W. van, 1996, A tomb of the First Dynasty at Tell Ibrahim Awad, *Oudheidkundige mededelingen uit het Rijksmuseum van Oudheden* 76, 7-34.

Haarlem, W. van, 1996, A remarkable 'hedgehog-ship' from Tell Ibrahim Awad, *Journal of Egyptian Archaeology* 82, 197-198.

Haarlem, W. van, 1996, Les établissements archaïques en Basse-Égypte orientale, *Les dossiers d'archéologie* 213, 12-15.

1995

Haarlem, W. van, 1995, Review of: Schlögl, H.A., Meves-Schlögl, C., 1993. Uschebti: Arbeiter im ägyptischen Totenreich. Wiesbaden, *Bibliotheca Orientalis* 52 (1-2), 62.

Haarlem, W. van, 1995, Temple deposits at Tell Ibrahim Awad: a preliminary report, *Göttinger Miszellen* 148, 45-52.

Haarlem, W. van, 1995, Een magische stèle uit Egypte, *Mededelingenblad. Vereniging van Vrienden Allard Pierson Museum* 62, 18-19.

Haarlem, W. van, 1995, *Allard Pierson Museum, Amsterdam, fascicle 3: stelae and reliefs. Corpus antiquitatum Aegyptiacarum: Lose-Blatt-Katalog ägyptischer Altertümer*. Amsterdam.

1994

Haarlem, W. van, 1994, De opgravingen op Tell Ibrahim Awad in 1993, *Phoenix* 40 (1), 33-43.

1993

Haarlem, W. van, 1993, Additions and corrections to the publication of a First Dynasty tomb from Tell Ibrahim Awad (eastern Nile Delta), *Göttinger Miszellen* 133, 37-52.

Haarlem, W. van, 1993, Vier stèles uit Kom Aboe Billoe, Egypte, *Mededelingenblad. Vereniging van Vrienden Allard Pierson Museum* 57, 14-16.

1992

Haarlem, W. van, 1992, A pair of papyrus sandals, *Journal of Egyptian Archaeology* 78, 294-295.

Haarlem, W. van, 1992, A functional analysis of ancient Egyptian amulets, in Anonymous (ed.), *Sesto Congresso internazionale di egittologia: atti 1*, Torino, 237-240.

1991

Haarlem, W. van, 1991, Een 'filistijns' sarcofaagfragment, *Mededelingenblad. Vereniging van Vrienden Allard Pierson Museum* 51, 24-25.

Haarlem, W. van, 1991, *Egypte. Kosmos kunstreisgidsen*. Utrecht.

1990

Haarlem, W. van, 1990, *Allard Pierson Museum, Amsterdam, fascicle 2: shabtis. Corpus antiquitatum Aegyptiacarum: Lose-Blatt-Katalog ägyptischer Altertümer*. Amsterdam.

Haarlem, W. van, 1990, Were the archaic kings buried in Sakkara or Abydos? *Discussions in Egyptology* 17, 73-74.

1989

Haarlem, W. van, 1989, Een curieuze vervalsing, *Mededelingenblad. Vereniging van Vrienden Allard Pierson Museum* 45, 24-25.

1988

Haarlem, W. van, 1988, Aegyptiaca diversa, *Mededelingenblad. Vereniging van Vrienden Allard Pierson Museum* 43, 35-36.

Haarlem, W. van, 1988, De Egyptische staatsgodsdienst, *Mededelingenblad. Vereniging van Vrienden Allard Pierson Museum* 44, 8-16.

Haarlem, W. van, 1988, Modern Egypt and its pharaonic heritage – a confrontation of two opinions, *Discussions in Egyptology* 11, 99-101.

1987

Haarlem, W. van, 1987, Stenen fragmenten uit Oxyrhynchus (Egypte), *Mededelingenblad. Vereniging van Vrienden Allard Pierson Museum* 41, 13-14.

Engel, E.-M., Haarlem, W. van, 1987, Review of: Herrmann, C., 1985, Formen für ägyptische Fayencen: Katalog der Sammlung des Biblischen Instituts der Universität Freiburg Schweiz and einer Privatsammlung. Orbis Biblicus et Orientalis 60. Freiburg (Schweiz); Göttingen, *Bibliotheca Orientalis* 44 (1-2), 143-145.

1986

Haarlem, W. van, Lunsingh Scheurleer, R.A., 1986, *Gids voor de afdeling Egypte*. Leiden.

Haarlem, W. van, Lunsingh Scheurleer, R.A., 1986, Gids voor de afdeling Egypte, *Phoenix* 32 (1), 1-121.

Haarlem, W. van, 1986 (ed.), *Allard Pierson Museum, Amsterdam, fascicle 1: selection from the collection. Corpus antiquitatum Aegyptiacarum: Lose-Blatt-Katalog ägyptischer Altertümer*. Amsterdam.

Haarlem, W. van, 1985-1986, Pottery from Sedment, Abydos and Qau in the Allard Pierson Museum, Amsterdam, *Jaarbericht van het Vooraziatisch-Egyptisch Genootschap Ex Oriente Lux* 29, 84-97.

1985

Haarlem, W. van, 1985, Evaluatie van "eender en anders", *Mededelingenblad. Vereniging van Vrienden Allard Pierson Museum* 33, 20-21.

Haarlem, W. van, 1985, Een koninklijke familie in het museum, *Mededelingenblad. Vereniging van Vrienden Allard Pierson Museum* 35, 14-15.

1982

Haarlem, W. van, 1981-1982, A rediscovered coffin-board of the First Intermediate Period, *Jaarbericht van het Vooraziatisch-Egyptisch Genootschap Ex Oriente Lux* 27, 29-32.

1978

Haarlem, W. van, 1978, Sjawabti's uit de Collectie Dobber, *Mededelingenblad. Vereniging van Vrienden Allard Pierson Museum* 15, 3-4.

1977

Haarlem, W. van, 1977, Een Egyptische stèle van Ramses I, *Mededelingenblad. Vereniging van Vrienden Allard Pierson Museum* 13, 6.

Haarlem, W. van, 1977, Een Fragment van een Egyptisch Tempelreliëf, *Mededelingenblad. Vereniging van Vrienden Allard Pierson Museum* 14, 10.

1976

Brink, E.C.M. van den, Haarlem, W. van, 1976, Enkele voorwerpen uit een Egyptische collectie. Schenking mevrouw B. Boeke-Cadbury, *Mededelingenblad Vereniging van Vrienden Allard Pierson Museum* 11, 1-7.

Tabula gratulatoria

Peter Akkermans
Professor Near Eastern Archaeology, Leiden University

Tine Bagh
Curator Egyptian Art, Ny Carlsberg Glyptotek, Copenhagen

Rob Demarée
Affiliated Fellow, Leiden Institute for Area Studies, Leiden University

Claire Derriks
Curator Emeritus Musée Royal de Mariemont, Professor Emeritus, Royal Institute of History of Art and Archaeology, Brussels

Koen Donker van Heel
Lecturer in Demotic, Abnormal Hieratic, and Ancient Egyptian Law, Institute for Area Studies, Leiden University

Christian Greco
Director Museo Egizio, Turin

Ben Haring
Senior University Lecturer Egyptology, Institute for Area Studies, Leiden University

Petra Hogenboom-Meijerink
Assistant Curator Egyptian Collections, National Museum of Antiquities, Leiden

Salima Ikram
Distinguished University Professor, Egyptology Unit Head, American University in Cairo

Jorrit Kelder
Grant Development, Leiden University

Olaf Kaper
Professor of Egyptology, Institute for Area Studies, Leiden University

Alexei Krol
Lomonosov Moscow State University, Anuchin Research Institute and Museum of Anthropology, Moscow

Ron Leenheer
Metals Conservator Allard Pierson, retired

Christian E. Loeben
Curator Egyptian and Islamic Collections, Museum August Kestner, Hannover

Marleen De Meyer
Assistant Director for Archaeology/ Egyptology, Netherlands-Flemish Institute in Cairo

Lars Petersen
Ausstellungskoordination Direktion, Badisches Landesmuseum

in: Bercken, B.J.L. van den, 2021. *Egyptian Delta archaeology. Short studies in honour of Willem van Haarlem*, Leiden: Sidestone Press, pp. 21-22.

Daniela Picchi
Curator Egyptian Collection, Museo Civico Archeologico, Bologna

Gabi Pieke
Curator Ancient Egypt, Reiss-Engelhorn Museen, Mannheim

Arnaud Quertinmont
Curator Egyptian and Near Eastern Antiquities, Musée Royal de Mariemont

Maarten Raven
Egyptologist, Honorary Research Associate at the National Museum of Antiquities, Leiden

Jerome C. Rose
University Professor Emeritus of Anthropology, University of Arkansas

Daniel Soliman
Curator Egyptian Collections, National Museum of Antiquities, Leiden

Alice Stevenson
Associate Professor Museum Studies, University College London, Institute of Archaeology

René van Walsem
University Lecturer, Egyptology, Institute for Area Studies, Leiden University

Lara Weiss
Curator Egyptian Collections, National Museum of Antiquities, Leiden

Harco Willems
Professor of Egyptology, KU Leuven

Willem van Haarlem, an appreciation

Manfred Bietak

It was after the World Conference of Egyptology at Grenoble in 1979 that Willem, together with his fellow student Edwin van den Brink, arrived at Tell el-Dab'a for the first time. I remember it was one of the few rainy days in the Delta in early September. From this season onwards we had a Dutch section within our team; it was later strengthened by Mario de Bruyn, who regrettably passed away a few years later, after the Dutch team had established an excavation of their own at Tell Ibrahim Awad.

Willem stayed with us the longest and contributed in a steady and efficient manner to the endeavours of our team. Later he took over the directorship of the Dutch excavations at Tell Ibrahim Awad from his colleague and early teammate Edwin van den Brink. There he was able to form an efficient team, our Dieter Eigner among them. The staffs of Tell Ibrahim Awad and of Tell el-Dab'a used to visit each other during the parallel seasons and such excursions were valuable for widening the horizons of students and scholars in both teams.

The chief discovery at Tell Ibrahim Awad was a stratigraphic series of temples from dynasty 0 until the Middle Kingdom. An important part of this discovery was the numerous deposits of ex-votos which compared well with other sites in Upper Egypt, such as the evidence from the Satet Temple on Elephantine Island and the temples at Hierakonpolis and Abydos.

Willem published an enduring and comprehensive study of ex-voto deposits from early temples in Egypt and the Levant. The early series of the Tell Ibrahim Awad temples proved to be of Near Eastern design and fitted in the temple development in the southern Levant in the Early Bronze II to III Period. After a series of broad-room temples the layout was changed to a bent-axis temple in the 4th to 5th dynasty. Such a shift can also be observed at Bab edh-Dhra' and Khirbet el-Batrawy in Jordan between the Early Bronze II and Early Bronze III Periods. This development probably went hand in hand with a change of religious practices in the southern Levant and proves that Tell Ibrahim Awad was not only a part of the Egyptian culture of the Early Dynastic Period and Old Kingdom but at the same time connected to the world of the Early Bronze Age in the Levant. This changes our perception of ancient Egypt during the Old Kingdom, which culturally speaking was much more open to its neighbours than hitherto envisaged.

in: Bercken, B.J.L. van den, 2021. *Egyptian Delta archaeology. Short studies in honour of Willem van Haarlem*, Leiden: Sidestone Press, pp. 23-25.

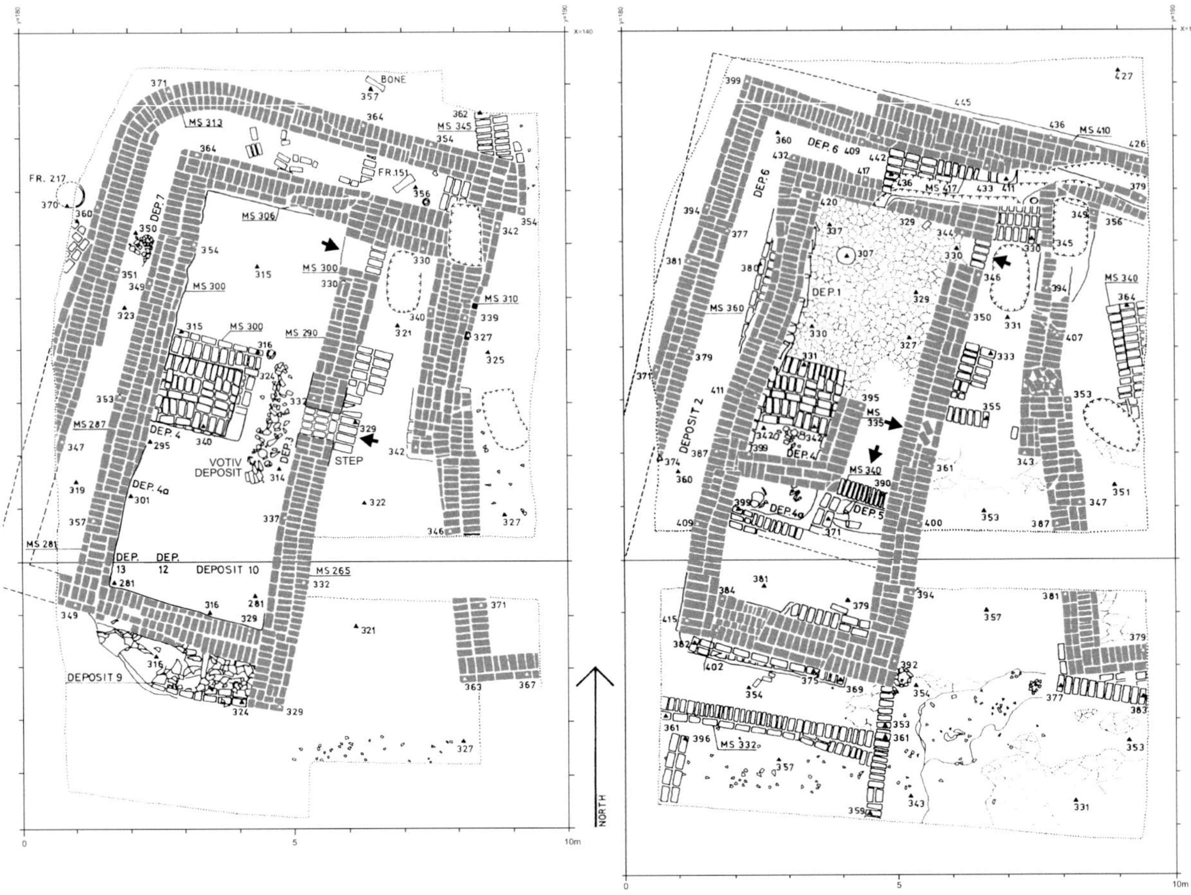

Fig. 1 The temple of Tell Ibrahim Awad (*c.*2600-2400 BC) was changed from a broad-room temple (left) to a bent-axis temple (right) as part of a temple restructuring programme seen in the southern Levant in the EB III, comparable to that at Khirbet el-Batrawy and Bab edh-Dhra' in Jordan. New interpretation of the archaeological evidence by Manfred Bietak (after Eigner 2000, figs. 2-3).

It is a pity that these important excavations cannot be continued for the time being, as land reclamation is taking its toll. The evidence that Willem van Haarlem and his team have so far collected at this site will, however, remain a valuable contribution to Egyptian archaeology and we all would like to wish Willem much success, joy and good health for his continued scholarly activity.

Bibliography

Eigner, D., 2000, Tell Ibrahim Awad: divine residence from Dynasty 0 until Dynasty 11, *Ägypten und Levante* 10, 17-36.

About the author

Manfred Bietak is emeritus professor at the Institute of Egyptology of the University of Vienna, founder and former director of the Austrian Archaeological Institute in Cairo and former director of the Vienna Institute of Archaeological Science. He directed excavations in Nubia (1961-1965), in Tell el-Dab'a (1966-2009 and 2011), in western Thebes (1969-1978) and in Bubastis (2012-2015). At present he is project leader and principal investigator for the ERC Advanced Grant *The Enigma of the Hyksos* at the Austrian Academy of Sciences. He is an elected member of nine academies of sciences and of three other scientific institutions. Bietak has authored, co-authored and edited numerous books and over 250 articles. He is the editor-in-chief of the journal *Egypt and the Levant*. He has also created an archaeological field school and supervised and led many students to graduation and academic careers.

Tell el-Iswid

A predynastic settlement in the eastern Delta

Béatrix Midant-Reynes and Nathalie Buchez

Introduction

Tell el-Iswid constitutes a key site for the understanding of the predynastic period in Egypt. This is a crucial phase of socio-economic transformations that took place during the fourth millennium BC and gave rise to a unified kingdom at the beginning of the third millennium BC. The site provides a wide range of interests. For many years, research on this period focused on the necropolises of Upper Egypt, leaving many questions about the settlements unanswered. The Delta was long considered a hostile land of swamps, unfit for human occupancy, until surveys and excavations carried out in the second half of the twentieth century brought to light many sites dating back to the first half of the fourth millennium BC (*c.*3800-3500 BC). They had enough similar cultural traits to be included in a cultural whole: the Lower-Egyptian Culture.[1] At this time structured communities lived in the Delta; their dwellings were located on the *gezira*, sandy hills that stayed dry during the annual floods that transformed the Delta into a large lake. In the sandy region of Upper Egypt, settlements often consist of vast areas of debris. The situation is different in the Delta, where the sedimentary environment led to the conservation of *stratified* sites. This is a considerable advantage when considering the succession of human habitation. The expansion throughout Egypt of the Upper-Egyptian cultural traits (Naqada) from 3500 BC onwards and the disappearance of the LEC in favour of the Naqadian from 3300 BC onwards is a crucial issue that is now much discussed among researchers.[2] Tell el-Iswid offers these three advantages: a domestic context on a stratified site that covers a period of cultural change that is still difficult to understand.

---

1 First called 'Maadi-Buto' because these two sites were at the origin of the discovery of this group of cultures. Since many others have been discovered throughout the Delta, the name LEC is preferred.

2 Midant-Reynes/Buchez 2019.

in: Bercken, B.J.L. van den, 2021. *Egyptian Delta archaeology. Short studies in honour of Willem van Haarlem*, Leiden: Sidestone Press, pp. 27-32.

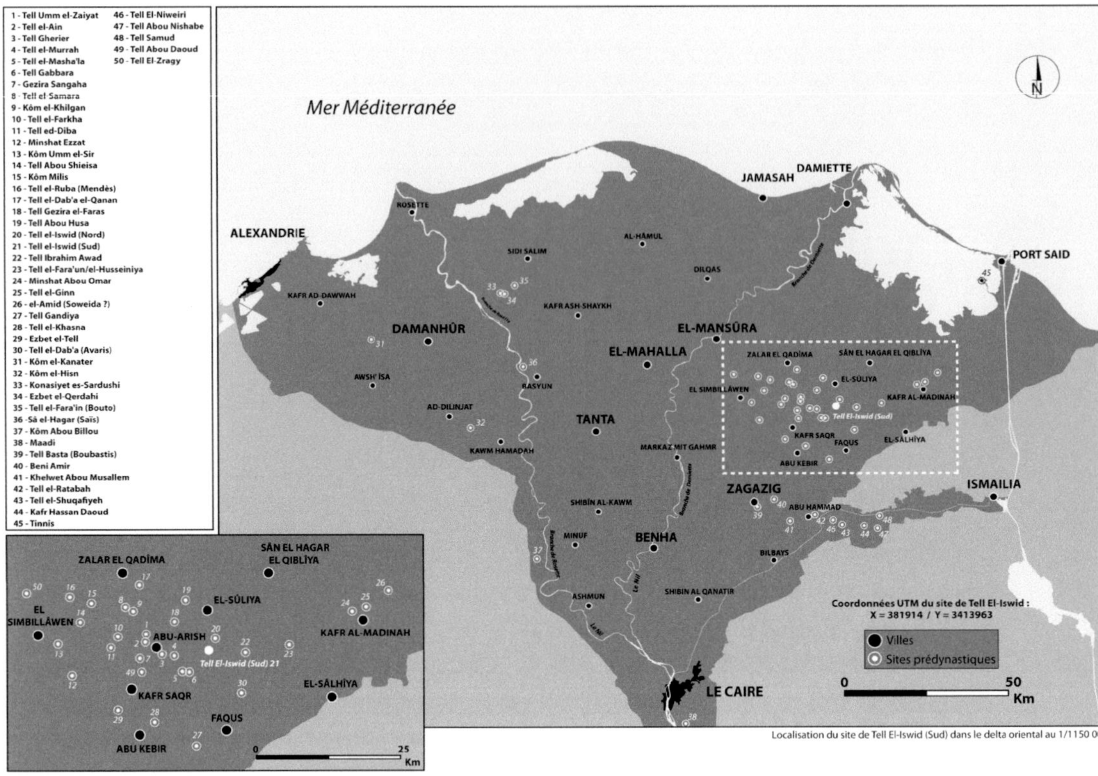

Fig. 1 Location of Tell el-Iswid among the predynastic sites of the Eastern Delta. Image J. Cavero/B. Fabry/F. Vinolas.

Renewed investigations

Tell el-Iswid, situated in Sharqiya Province, 14 km north-west of Faqus and 6 km south-east of Tell Râk (fig. 1), is a neighbouring site of Tell Ibrahim Awad in the eastern Delta. It was only discovered in 1987 during deep coring surveys and soundings conducted by a team from the University of Amsterdam.[3] It is located on a mound of 400 x 300 m (fig. 2) and is surrounded on all sides by irrigation channels and fields. Despite recent disturbances (the central part has been used as agricultural land since the 1960s) it is relatively well preserved.

The Dutch mission carried out two limited soundings, which highlighted the existence of a stratified settlement with domestic features and associated objects. Two main predynastic phases were identified. The earlier shows affinities with the Lower-Egyptian Culture (Iswid A); the upper levels belong to the Naqada III-Early Dynastic Period (Iswid B). So from the start Tell el-Iswid appeared as a major site for the study of the fourth millennium BC in the Nile Delta.

In 2006, a new multi-disciplinary programme was initiated by the French Institute for Oriental Archaeology (IFAO).[4] It planned to integrate the study of the Tell el-Iswid site

3 Van den Brink 1989.
4 Led by B. Midant-Reynes (2006-2016), then by N. Buchez (since 2016).

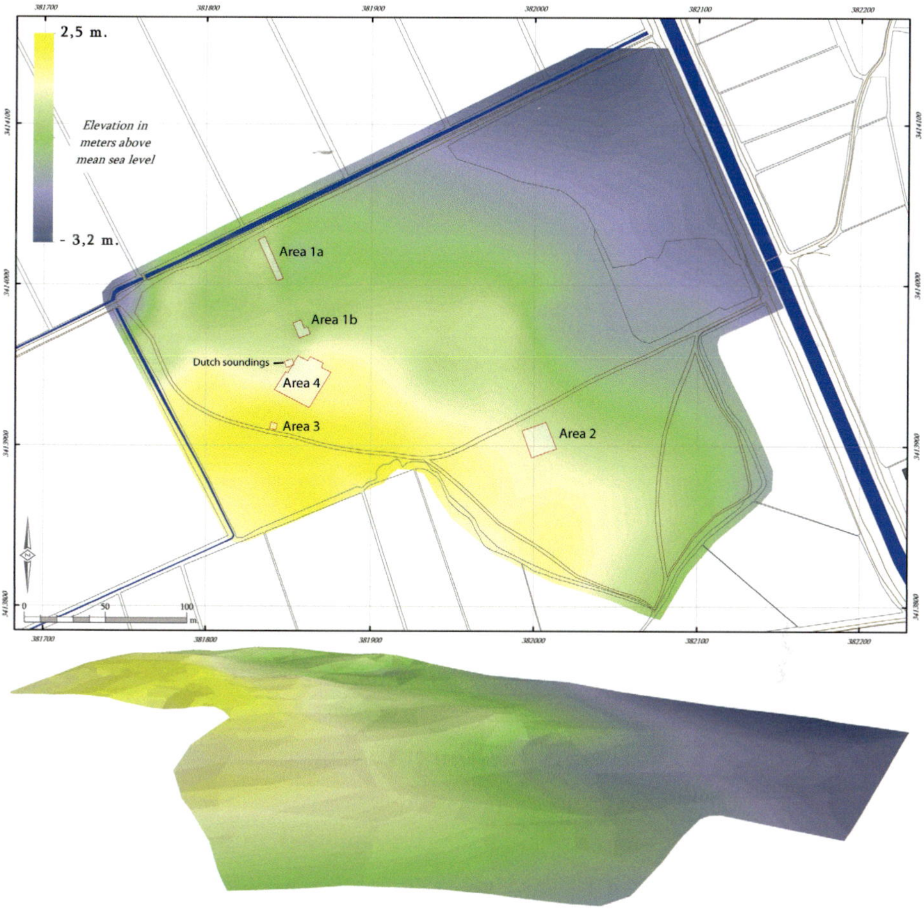

Fig. 2 Digital Elevation Model of the Pleistocene sands of the *gezira* with location of the excavated areas. Image J. Cavero/B. Fabry/F. Vinolas.

into a project that investigated the interactions between humans and the environment.[5] The aim of this project was to determine the archaeological potential of the site and to investigate the ancient topography of the location, again by means of core drilling and archaeological soundings, now in combination with magnetic surveys.

Results

The data obtained shows that the *tell*, which today covers about 8 ha, is only part of a site that extends over a vast sandy area (a *gezira*) now covered by agricultural fields.[6] A section of 30 m long was opened along an existing cut in order to establish a reference stratigraphy. It confirms that the first human settlements on the *tell* date back to the beginning of the fourth millennium BC and cover the whole millennium. It also suggests that a final phase

5 Project called ANR-Gezira (Agence Nationale de la Recherche).

6 A first monography was published: Midant-Reynes/Buchez 2014. A second volume is in preparation. See also Midant-Reynes et al. 2014.

Fig. 3 Tell el-Iswid Area 4. The Naqadian mud-brick building in the last phase of occupancy. View from the south (image R. el-Hajaoui).

of extensive habitation took place during the Late Period, while there are also occasional indications of a moderate presence during the 4th dynasty, 11th dynasty, the end of the Second Intermediate Period and the beginning of the New Kingdom.

The original topography of the *gezira* as revealed by the core drilling is quite different from the current topography (fig. 2). The annual flood caused destruction in the lower parts of the *gezira*, leading the inhabitants to make successive reconstructions which finally caused accumulations in these areas. As a result the current topography is inverted:[7] what was originally at the top of the sandy mound is now located below.

The combined data of excavation and core drilling allowed us to attain the first goal of achieving the best possible image of the site's stratigraphic sequences, but the question of how to detect areas where there is a high probability of finding predynastic structures on the 8 ha of the *tell* remained open. Magnetic surveying was adopted to answer this question. In 2009 a magnetic survey was undertaken over a large part of the *tell*.[8] It allowed us to clearly identify the remains of a rectangular structure with several inner spaces, located in the western part of the site. Excavations were then undertaken at this location (area 4) from 2010 to 2014. They brought to light a mud-brick building,[9] of which several construction phases have been highlighted (fig. 3). It dates from Naqada IIIA2-B, as evidenced by the ceramic material and a sherd engraved with the name of Iry-Hor.[10] Over

7 Buchez/Cavero 2014, fig.3.
8 Led by T. Herbich.
9 Midant-Reynes/Buchez (eds.), forthcoming.
10 Midant-Reynes 2019.

Fig. 4 Tell el-Iswid Area 4. Remains of calcified wood in the trenches. Image mission Tell el-Iswid/R. el Hajaoui.

time, the stable plots of land in this area are increasingly filled up with buildings. Domestic units are getting more and more complex and consist of a greater number of rooms.

Levels previous to the Naqada buildings correspond to an impressive succession of narrow trenches and small pits belonging to the Lower Egyptian Culture (first part of the fourth millennium BC), as is shown by the ceramic material. These trenches and pits bear witness to the architecture of walls and palisades made of light materials, which make up multi-roomed units. Indeed, remains of calcified wood unearthed in these trenches indicate lightly built structures with vertical elements (a kind of trellis, fig. 4). This type of construction requires regular maintenance. As a result, the trenches are more or less superimposed, making it difficult to identify each of them during excavation. This kind of building develops over a stratigraphic depth of around 1.5 m, representing 200 to 300 years of occupancy. An evolutionary pattern can be observed in the middle of the sequence, however, with the appearance of a large number of silos, which seem to indicate an increase in storage capacity and the development of more intensive cereal agriculture. Shortly afterwards, in the final stage of the Lower-Egyptian Culture, a new architectural tradition using mud brick emerged, very likely linked to the intensifying trade between the Delta and the Nile valley as indicated by the increase of imported items.

Archaeological research in the Delta over the past twenty years has significantly altered our understanding of the Lower-Egyptian Culture. Stratified sites such as Buto in the western Delta, Tell el-Farkha or Tell Ibrahim Awad in the eastern Delta have provided first-hand documentation of both the architecture and the associated materials (ceramics, lithics, grindstones) in their stratigraphic, economic and environmental context. With other sites, Tell el-Iswid feeds the debate on the question of the great social transformations of the fourth millennium BC.

Bibliography

Brink, E.C.M. van den, 1989, A transitional Late Predynastic-Early Dynastic settlement site in the northeastern Nile Delta, Egypt, *Mitteilungen des Deutschen Archäologischen Instituts, Abteilung Kairo* 45, 55-108.

Buchez, N., Cavero, J., 2014, Premières données sur l'évolution générale de la topographie du Tell, in Midant-Reynes, B., Buchez, N. (eds.), 2014, *Tell el Iswid. 2006-2009. Fouilles de l'Institut Français d'Archéologie Orientale* 73, Le Caire, 11-15.

Midant-Reynes, B., 2019, Une nouvelle attestation d'Iry-Hor dans le Delta : Tell el-Iswid, in Vuillemier, S., Meyrat, P. (eds.), 2019, *Sur les pistes du désert. Mélanges offerts à Michel Valloggia*, Infolio editions, Gollion, 155-169.

Midant-Reynes, B., Buchez, N. (eds.), 2014, *Tell el Iswid. 2006-2009. Fouilles de l'Institut Français d'Archéologie Orientale* 73, Le Caire.

Midant-Reynes, B., Buchez, N., 2019, Naqadian Expansion : A Review of the Question based on the Necropolis of Kom el-Khilgan, *ArchéoNil* 29, 129-156.

Midant-Reynes, B., Buchez, N., Bréand, G., Briois, F., Cavero, J., Coupey, A.S., Dapper, M. De, Delhopital, N., Emery-Barbier, A., el-Hajaoui, R., Guérin, S., Guyot, F., Hochstrasser-Petit, C., Lesur, J., Minotti, M., Regulski, I., Robitaille, J., Torchy, L., Tristant, Y., 2014, Tell el-Iswid 2006-2010. The Archaeology of the Eastern Nile Delta in the 4th millenium BC, *Aegyptus est imago caeli, Studies Presented to Krzysztof M. Cialowicz on His 60th Birthday*, Krakow, 37-56.

Midant-Reynes, B., Buchez, N. (eds.), forthcoming. *Tell el-Iswid 2010-2014. Les occupations naqadiennes du secteur 4. Fouilles de l'Institut Français d'Archéologie Orientale*, Le Caire.

About the authors

Béatrix Midant-Reynes has specialised in the study of Egyptian prehistory. For the IFAO, she has directed the excavation of several predynastic sites in Egypt: Adaïma in Upper Egypt (necropolis and settlement), Kom el-Khilgan in the Eastern Delta (necropolis), Tell el-Iswid in the eastern Delta (settlement). In 2015, she handed over the direction of the Tell el-Iswid excavation to Nathalie Buchez. From 2000 to 2015, she co-directed the prehistory section of the prospecting programme in the southern basin of Douch (Kharga oasis). From 2010 to 2015, she was director of the French Institute of Oriental Archaeology. She is currently emeritus research director at the CNRS. Among her published works, two are addressed to a wider public: *Prehistory of Egypt: From the First Egyptians to the First Pharaohs*, London 2000, and *Les origines de l'Égypte. Du Néolithique à l'émergence de l'État*, Paris 2003.

Nathalie Buchez is head of archaeological research at Inrap (Institut national de recherche en archéologie préventive). She is in charge of field operations, ceramic studies and project coordination concerning the Bronze and Early Iron Ages in northern France. With a PhD in archaeology from the EHESS, attached to the UMR 5608-TRACES of Toulouse, she has been carrying out research on predynastic Egypt since 1989. In 2015, she succeeded Béatrix Midant-Reynes as head of the Tell el-Iswid excavation (eastern Delta) for the IFAO and the Ministry of Europe and Foreign Affairs. She has published numerous articles relating to predynastic Egypt and is the author of a thesis on the evolution of settlement in Adaïma (Upper Egypt) based on the analysis of ceramic and archaeological data.

'A curious feature was the presence of several ivory or bone rods.'

Ancient mikado or something completely different?

Vincent Boele

Introduction

In 1995 I was a member of the team excavating and researching the site at Tell Ibrahim Awad in the eastern Nile Delta. In that season a number of deposit pits were found under the floor of the temple in area A. Many different objects were discovered, including a few bundles of thin ivory sticks found in deposit pit no. 4 (fig. 1). Unfortunately these sticks were never counted, properly cleaned, conserved or documented. In his thesis Willem writes about them: 'a curious feature was the presence of several ivory or bone rods.' In a footnote he suggests that they are 'possibly thin gaming rods'.[1] Here I would like to explore this hypothesis.

Games in Egypt

Were there any games in ancient Egypt that could be linked to these sticks? Pharaonic Egypt had a limited number of (board) games: *mehen*, named after the snake goddess, was played using a circular board in the shape of a snake. It dates back to predynastic times and was popular until the end of the Old Kingdom.[2] *Senet* and *aseb*, also known as 'Twenty Squares', were two similar games which often consisted of a box with a playing field of small squares and an inner compartment used for storing the gaming pieces. The same box could have a *senet* and an *aseb* side. The oldest depiction of a *senet* game was found in the *mastaba* of Hesy-Re in the necropolis of Saqqara (Old Kingdom, *c.*2620 BC), while even older gaming pieces and *senet* boards have been excavated at Abu Rawash in a 1st-dynasty *mastaba* dating to the reign of King Dewen, around 3000 BC.[3] *Aseb*, originally from Persia and also known as the 'Royal Game' in Ur, came to

---

1 Van Haarlem 2014, 54 footnote 40. I would like to thank Ben van den Bercken for his help in the research for this article.

2 See https://www.ucl.ac.uk/museums-static/digitalegypt//naqada/gameboard.html.

3 See Piccione 2007, 54. A beautiful fragment of a *senet* board is kept in the Arizona State Museum, ASM 12496; see Romano et al. 2018, 74-77.

in: Bercken, B.J.L. van den, 2021. *Egyptian Delta archaeology. Short studies in honour of Willem van Haarlem*, Leiden: Sidestone Press, pp. 33-38.

Fig. 1 Photo of deposit 4, where the ivory sticks can be seen *in situ* (image from https://easy.dans.knaw.nl/ui/datasets/id/easy-dataset:87581/tab/2).

the Levant around the third millennium BC and was most popular in ancient Egypt from the Second Intermediate Period onwards.[4] Both games were related to the journey into the afterlife and played with small conical pieces and cylindrical, biconcave ones. Last but not least is the 'Game of Hounds and Jackals'. This game used ten slightly conical sticks ending in two different types of canine heads (five per type). The Metropolitan Museum of Art in New York has a wonderful example of this game with beautifully carved heads.[5] These are traditionally interpreted as hounds and jackals, but probably they are two types of dogs, one with pointed ears, the other with hanging ears. But that is another discussion.

Are there other possibilities for the use of the sticks in board games? The Egyptians used long sticks as dice. These casting sticks, used in groups of four to six pieces, have a flat and a rounded side. After they were thrown into the air and landed, the number of sticks with the flat side up told the player how many places they could move on the gaming board.[6] But the sticks found in Tell Ibrahim Awad were round and longer (approximately 30 to 40 cm long) and showed no visible decoration. Therefore Van Haarlem's conclusion that these are gaming rods seems unlikely.

The ivory sticks

But what could they otherwise be? Could they be related to the numerous mace heads that were found in the same deposit no. 4? Many mace heads in this find complex have biconcave drilled holes which allow for fixing thin rods in them. The sticks used in maces were made of wood, horn or ivory.[7] The openings that are left after the stick is inserted can be filled with wood or another material to fix the mace head, or – as Wolfgang Decker suggests – with a leather strap.[8] Similar fastenings can be found in African maces and in Oceania.[9]

The mace heads that were found in deposit 4 are all made of stone. Most of them are ovoid while some are disc-shaped. As is typical they all have a central perforation hole, often drilled from two sides (biconcave) which makes it possible to create a strong joint with the handle.

Maces and mace heads were used in the ancient Near East, Levant and Egypt somewhere in the course of the fourth millennium BC.[10] One of the most famous depictions of a mace head can be found on the Narmer Palette, dating back to 3200-3000 BC (fig. 2). On the palette we see King Narmer slaying a Libyan enemy with a mace that consists of a relatively small mace head and a stick that flares toward the end. It seems that maces in predynastic and early Egyptian times played an important (ceremonial) role, since a few

---

4 See https://www.metmuseum.org/exhibitions/listings/2014/assyria-to-iberia/blog/posts/twenty-squares; see also the *senet*/Twenty Squares board box found in Thebes, now in the Metropolitan Museum New York, inv. 16.10.475a.

5 See https://www.metmuseum.org/art/collection/search/543867.

6 See Piccione 2007, 56; https://www.metmuseum.org/art/collection/search/559441; the British Museum in London has a few similar sticks: https://www.britishmuseum.org/collection/object/Y_EA20935.

7 Decker 1982, 414.

8 Decker 1982, 414.

9 Cp. a mace from the Baining people and the Gunantuna people (Gazelle Peninsula, Papua New Guinea) in which the mace head is fixed with rattan fibres. MAS Antwerp, inventory number AE.1955.0028.0289.1-2; https://search.mas.be/Details/collect/132020.

10 Wengrow 2006, 52-53.

Fig. 2 Recto side of the Narmer Palette, Egypt, siltstone, 62 x 42 cm, *c.*3200-3000 BC, Egyptian Museum, Cairo CG 14716. The palette was found in the ancient city of Nekhen, also known as Hierakonpolis (image Wikimedia Commons, CC-PD-M 1.0).

Fig. 3 Club of the Nilotic Maasai people, Tanzania, horn, 55.7 x 6.1 cm (head), before 1940, City of Antwerp Collection, MAS AE.7149. Image MAS.

giant mace heads have been found, decorated with reliefs depicting two of Egypt's earliest kings, Scorpion and Narmer.[11] These oversized mace heads were purely ritual and ceremonial. The original, smaller stone maces were weapons as well as typical grave gifts during the predynastic period.[12]

Maces like this are also found in more recent civilisations, such as the people of the Nilotic Maasai tribe in Kenya-Tanzania (fig. 3).[13] The mace heads are just as small as the Egyptian ones and the sticks are relatively thin, though slightly larger in size because they also served as ceremonial staffs. Is it possible that, parallel to these modern examples, the ivory rods from Tell Ibrahim Awad could be the sticks that once served as the handles of the mace heads in pit no. 4? They were found in the same pit, not far from the mace heads. The size of the rods and the holes in the mace heads seem to be in line with one another. Once fixed to one another they would strongly resemble the depictions of maces like in the Narmer Palette. Perhaps they were separated in the deposit to symbolically break their power. Unfortunately, as I said before, the sticks were never cleaned, nor were they placed in the mace heads to see if they would fit. But in my opinion they belong to the mace heads. Ivory or bone is a very useful material for this purpose because these sticks can be thin but strong. With the mace head at one end of the stick an effective centre of gravity is created. Combined with the heavier mace head a thin ivory stick has the ability to deliver a very powerful blow when used as a melee weapon. The more flexible the stick, the harder the blow – a hard blow delivered with such a mace can easily kill an enemy with one strike. They could also serve as throwing weapons, since the heavier mace head gives the weapon an enormous speed when thrown. In short, it is a very effective hand weapon.

Bibliography

Decker, Wolfgang, 1982, Keule, in Helck, W., 1982, *Lexikon der Ägyptologie*, Band 3, 413-414.

Haarlem, Willem van, 2014, *Temple Deposits in Early Dynastic Egypt: The Case of Tell Ibrahim Awad*, Leiden.

Piccione, Peter A. 2007. 'The Egyptian game of senet and the migration of the soul'. In Finkel, Irving L. (ed.), *Ancient board games in perspective: papers from the 1990 British Museum colloquium*, 54-63. London: British Museum Press.

Romano, Irene Bald, William John Tait, Christina Bisulca, Pearce Paul Creasman, Gregory Hodgins, and Tomasz Wazny, 2018. An ancient Egyptian senet board

11 The so-called Narmer Mace Head (inv. no. E.3631), Major (E.3632) and Minor Scorpion Mace Head, all kept in the Ashmolean Museum in Oxford, England.

12 Wengrow 2006, 52-53.

13 The Maasai are a nomadic Nilotic tribe, living in Kenya and Tanzania, south of Egypt. They are shepherds with large cattle. Their tunics, red cloaks and weapons are sometimes thought to have been influenced by the uniforms and weapons of Roman soldiers. Their colourful collars resemble Egyptian examples.

in the Arizona State Museum. *Zeitschrift für ägyptische Sprache und Altertumskunde* 145 (1), 71-85

Wengrow David, 2006. *The archaeology of Early Egypt. Social Transformations in North-East Africa, 10,000 to 2650 BC*. Cambridge, Cambridge University Press.

About the author

Vincent Boele is an art historian specialising in classical archaeology and Egyptology. During his career he has worked on a wide range of projects. After working for the Allard Pierson and the Bijbels Museum he became an exhibition curator for both the Nieuwe Kerk and Hermitage Amsterdam (2001-2019), collaborating intensively with the State Hermitage Museum in Saint Petersburg. Since 2019 he is working as curator World Cultures and exhibition curator at the MAS Museum in Antwerp. He has published many articles on various art historical topics.

An unusual ripple-flaked knife from Cemetery U at Abydos/Umm el-Qaab[1]

Thomas Hikade

Introduction

In 2000 I had the very great pleasure of working with Willem van Haarlem at Tell Ibrahim Awad, where I was able to study the full lithic sequence from the late fourth to the late third millennium BC. That site did not yield any ripple-flaked knives, but I would like to present a very interesting example from Cemetery U at Abydos in Upper Egypt. The context of this find may open up discussions about the nature of the use of these remarkable knives.

Egyptian predynastic ripple-flaked knives

Ripple-flaked knives are a tool category of predynastic Egypt used during the Naqada IID period (*c.*3500-3300 BC). They are characterised by visible remains of the grinding of the preform at the back and a very delicate retouching pattern on the front. After the grinding of the preform, flakes were removed in such a way that each new detached flake overlapped the previously detached flake. This created the impression of C-shaped flake scars. In the next step, the delta-shaped areas between these flakes were further retouched with a fine parallel pressure flaking. In the final step, a very fine serration (lambda retouching) was applied running along the cutting edge between the handle area and the curved tip of the knife. Ripple-flaked knives are considered 'some of the finest flint tools ever made'.[2]

Some of the knives can be rather big, such as a knife from Abu Zeidan Tomb 32 measuring 28.8 cm in length.[3] For some of the knives we still have their ivory handles

---

1 In 2000 I had the opportunity to work with Willem van Haarlem at Tell Ibrahim Awad and although there was no ripple-flaked knife, it allowed me to follow the stone-tool sequence of the site from Late Predynastic to the First Intermediate Period. It is a great honour for me to have been invited to contribute to Willem's *Festschrift*. I would like to thank Jane Roy, D'arne O'Neill, and Chloe Condie for their valuable contributions.

2 Wittaker 1994, 175.

3 Needler 1984, 124, 272-273. It is one of three ripple-flaked knives from this tomb. Needler dates the tomb to Naqada III, which makes these ripple-flaked knives the only ones dated after Naqada IId.

in: Bercken, B.J.L. van den, 2021. *Egyptian Delta archaeology. Short studies in honour of Willem van Haarlem*, Leiden: Sidestone Press, pp. 39-46.

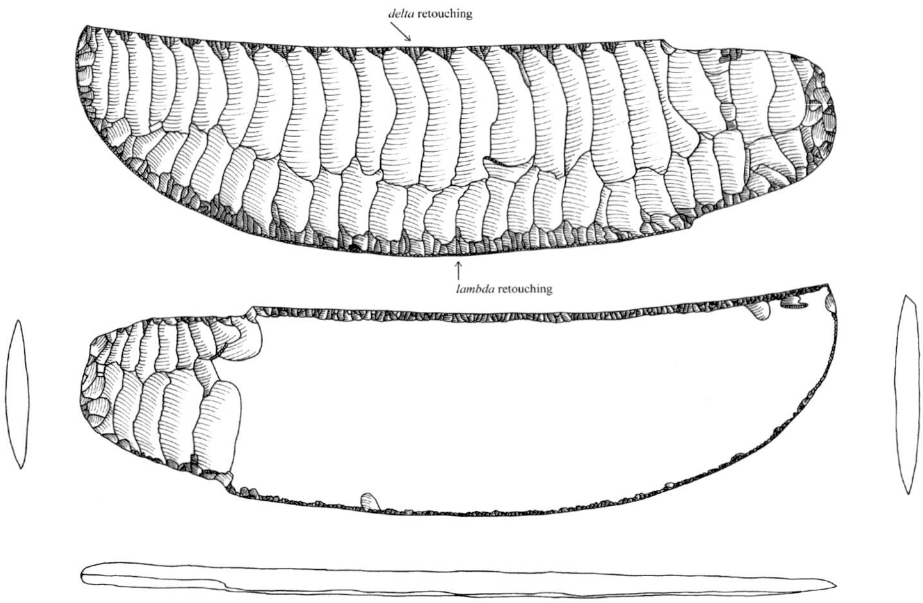

Fig. 1 Ripple-flaked knife from Tomb U-503 at Abydos (Umm el-Qaab) showing the fine C-shaped retouching and the lambda retouching at the cutting edge, and regular delta retouching at the back of the blade. The front is shown at the top of the drawing, the back at the bottom (image Thomas Hikade).

or remains thereof.[4] Some of the knives were deliberately broken, possibly during a funerary ritual.[5]

In an earlier study investigating six ripple-flaked knives housed at the Museum of Archaeology and Ethnology in Cambridge (UK), Bruce A. Bradley described the steps from the preform to the final product.[6] Later on Peter Kelterborn replicated several ripple-flaked knives detailing the various production steps (the so-called *chaîne opératoire*).[7] Altogether he identified six stages to obtain a finished ripple-flaked knife:

- Stage 1: Obtaining the blank (blanks about 20-30 cm long and 10-20 cm wide).
- Stage 2: Obtaining the percussion form (bifacial thinning of the blank with hard and soft percussion).
- Stage 3: Obtaining the grinding preform (grinding on sand or sandstone).
- Stage 4: Front surface flaking (precision flaking by pressure).
- Stage 5: Marginal retouching (extremely fine pressure flaking).
- Stage 6: Serration of cutting edge (extremely fine grinding and bifacial pressure flaking).

4 E.g. the Brooklyn knife, Needler 1984, 270, or the famous knife from Gebel el-Araq in the Louvre Museum. For the latter see Dreyer 1999, 218, fig. 4. Dreyer also discussed further fragments of handles from Cemetery U at Abydos and the reconstructed handle of the knife from Tomb U-503.

5 Scharff 1926, pl. 29.

6 Bradley 1972.

7 Kelterborn 1984. For his study he also analysed twelve ripple-flaked knives in European museums.

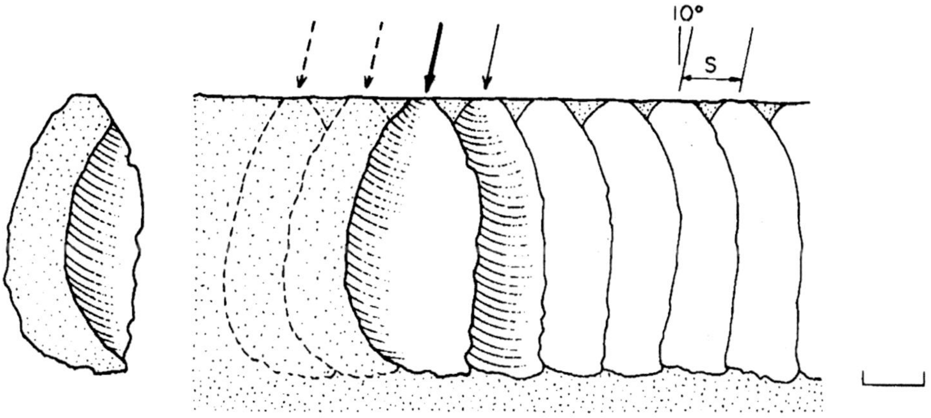

Fig. 2 The 'secret' of C-flaking (after Kelterborn 1984, fig. 6b).

Reluctantly, Kelterborn gives an estimated time to manufacture a ripple-flaked knife of less than twenty working hours, although time was certainly of no concern to the ancient flint-knapper. He also laments missing links of knives from various stages of the production. There might, however, be just such an unfinished knife for stage 4, where the C-flaking was left unfinished; it was found at Naqada.[8] In a seminal study Béatrix Midant-Reynes later combined Kelterborn's results with data about ripple-flaked knives from Egypt, the decorated ivory handles of some of them, and their status as elite objects.[9] Midant-Reynes looked into 29 archaeological sites totalling thousands of tombs to find that there are just 49 ripple-flaked knives. The richest site is Abusir el-Meleq with 15 knives. I compiled a list of ripple-flaked knives some years later including a few more recent finds from Egypt and knives that have come to museums via the art market and ended up with 74 knives. This clearly proves how rare these knives were.

The big ripple-flaked knife from Cemetery U

From 1970 the German Archaeological Institute in Cairo has re-excavated the royal tombs of the earliest kings of Egypt at Abydos in Middle Egypt.[10] The predynastic Cemetery U, located farther north, was fully excavated between 1985 and 2002. Cemetery U has around 650 tombs and covers the period from Naqada IA to Naqada III, which is almost the entire fourth millennium BC. Cemetery U was an elite cemetery, the youngest tombs lined with mud brick.[11]

The knife (find number Ab K 1101, register number 197, see fig. 3) was found on the surface between graves U-200 and U-127 in the southern section of Cemetery U. It is 31.5 cm long, 4.4 cm wide, and 0.7 cm thick. Its weight is 142 g. To date it is the biggest

8 Petrie 1896, pl. LXXIV, 81b.

9 Midant-Reynes 1987.

10 For references of the works carried out at the Royal Cemetery and Cemetery U, see Hartung 2016, 272.

11 The most famous of these brick-lined tombs is Tomb U-j with twelve underground chambers and a very rich inventory of finds, among them hundreds of foreign wine vessels. For the tomb see Dreyer 1998 and Hartung 2001.

ripple-flaked knife discovered.[12] The knife is made of light to mid-brown flint. It shows some light patina and weathered areas on both sides, which indicates that it once lay on the desert surface and was exposed to the elements for some time. Patination on flint is usually linked to water. That patina is not present on the retouches in the handle area on both sides. This could indicate that the handle was actually reworked at some stage.[13] Some areas still show traces of the grinding stage of the preform (left white in fig. 3). The lengthwise section has an elongated lens shape with an abrupt edge at the tip. The cross-section is also lens-shaped but shows a steep retouching at the tip of the cutting edge. With this it becomes clear that the knife was once used and reshaped. This is unusual because generally the cutting edges of ripple-flaked knives have a fine serration with hardly any damage, which seems to indicate that these knives were never used. On the upper margin are forty rather irregular C-flake scars. The middle line between the upper and lower retouches is quite irregular, which fits the observation by Kelterborn.[14] While there is delta retouching at the back of the knife, there are no remains of any lambda retouching along the cutting edge.

A possible archaeological context for the big ripple-flaked knife

As mentioned above, the knife was found on the surface between U-200 and U-127. Tomb U-200 in fact held the remains of two inventories: one that dates to Naqada IIA (*c.*3700 BC), which is the original context, and finds from Naqada IID2 (*c.*3400 BC), which can be considered intrusive. Tomb U-127 is dated to Naqada IID1-IID2 (*c.*3500-3400 BC). It is remarkable that in this tomb remains of five different handles for ripple-flaked knives were found.[15]

A photo of the ripple-flaked knife was first published in 1993 and the knife was tentatively associated with Tomb U-127.[16] This grave is a large rectangular pit (4.5 x 1.6 m, with a depth of approximately 1.8 m). Its southern part was disturbed completely and the northern part was disturbed to a great extent. It contained the remains of a wooden coffin and some bones of an adult. Some bones of cattle and sheep or goat were found in the pit filling. Among the non-ceramic finds are fragments of stone vessels and a piece of a calcite or alabaster mace. Unfired clay *bullae* (clay seal impressions) and fragments thereof, depicting heads of ibexes, fish, and boats were also found.[17]

Several fragments of one decorated and two undecorated ivory knife handles were also found on the floor at the southern end of the pit. One of the decorated fragments depicts a row of gift bearers going to the right with shoulder-length hair and dressed in long undecorated clothes. A second fragment shows a row of at least four kneeling captives led by a clearly naked standing captive, all beside an archer's bow and probably depicted with their arms tied behind their backs. Underneath is a row of male prisoners

---

12 The second in length is 30 cm without provenance and unpublished. It is in the Egyptian Museum in Cairo (JE 50060). The knives are generally between 20 and 26 cm.

13 A reworked ripple-flaked knife was already found earlier in the twentieth century, at Abydos. Naville 1914, pl. III, no. 3. Here the handle was clearly altered and is much smaller in width than the blade, while in our case the handle has maintained a balance in width of handle and blade.

14 Kelterborn 1984, fig. 7.

15 Dreyer 1999, 205-210.

16 Dreyer et al. 1993, pl. 6a.

17 Dreyer 1999, 205-210 fig. 10-11.

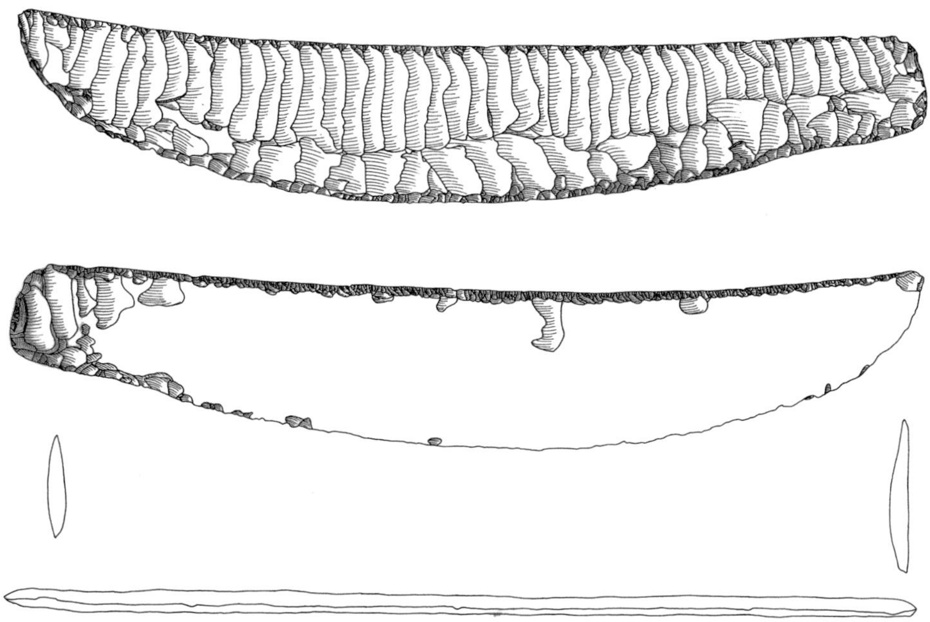

Fig. 3 Big ripple-flaked knife from Cemetery U at Abydos/Umm el-Qaab (image Thomas Hikade).

with guards and this time four men are squatting in front of them. All figures face to the right and all men are bearded. Both scenes tell a story of victory and defeat. Further fragments show animals such as lions, cattle, and caprids marching in a row. It seems possible that all these fragments belonged to one knife with the animals on the front and the humans on the back of the ivory handle.

Three other ivory fragments could be reconstructed as coming from a dagger handle.[18] The carving shows lions, gazelles, birds and dragons. Unfortunately, no flint or copper blade for the handles was found. The lithic assemblage from the tomb clearly confirms the high status of the person once buried here: twenty micro-endscrapers and one complete fishtail knife supplement a set of four simple bladelets.[19] As the former were all found close together it is most likely that they were once put into a small organic container, such as a leather pouch. The function of the micro-endscraper is still unknown but seems to be related to the exploitation of aquatic resources.[20] The most remarkable flint object from U-127 is certainly the bifacially retouched fishtail knife (Ab K 1102, R198, fig. 4). It was made of a light brown flint with pinkish stripes. It measures 14.9 x 5.8 x 0.7 cm and weighs 55 g. The retouching looks very similar to the technique used on the ripple-flaked knives. Apart from the lower section of the blade that was once fitted into a handle the whole edge of the blade is very finely serrated.

---

18 Hartung 2008, 185 fig. 2.

19 Hikade 1996, 135-139 fig. 6-7.

20 Schmidt 1993, 267-277.

Conclusion

So, to which tomb does the big ripple-flaked knife belong? It is clear that ripple-flaked knives are rare and must have belonged to the elite, possibly to the leaders of communities. It is also clear that none of the handle fragments from Tomb U-127 could be matched to our big ripple-flaked knife. It is moreover evident that the knife was exposed to the elements for some time. It was reworked and the blade re-sharpened. As there are no signs of ongoing ritual activities at Cemetery U, the knife must have been used in a settlement context. What kind of context – domestic, in public or ritual – cannot be confirmed. The evidence we do have, however, places the ripple-flaked knife outside the cemetery context to which they were thus far confined. It is now a stone tool used and reworked by the living.

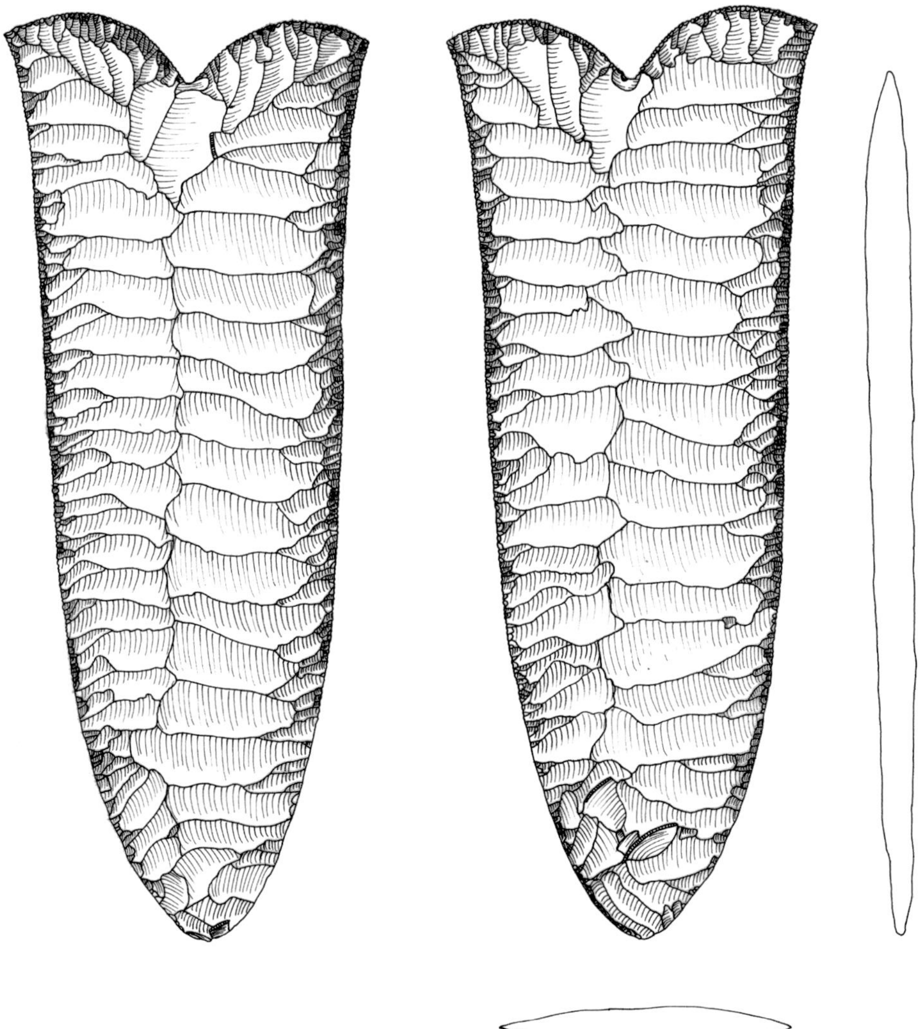

Fig. 4 Fishtail knife from Tomb U-127 (image Thomas Hikade).

Bibliography

Bradley, B.A., 1972, Predynastic Egyptian Flint Implements – An Inductive Technological Sequence, *Newsletter of Lithic Technology*, Vol. 1 No.3, 2-5.

Dreyer, G., 1998, Umm el-Qaab I. Das prädynastische Königsgrab U-j und seine frühen Schriftzeugnisse, *Archäologische Veröffentlichungen* 86, Mainz.

Dreyer, G., 1999, Motive und Datierung der dekorierten prädynastischen Messergriffe, Ziegler, C., Palayret, N. (eds.), 1999, *L'art de l'Ancien Egypt, Actes du colloque organise au musée du Louvre par le Service culturel les 3 et 4 avril 1998*, Paris, 195-226.

Dreyer, G., Hartung, U., Pumpenmeier, F., 1993, Umm el-Qaab. Nachuntersuchungen im frühzeitlichen Königsfriedhof 5./6. Vorbericht, *Mitteilungen des Deutschen Archäologischen Instituts Kairo* 49, 23-62.

Hartung, U., 2001, Umm el-Qaab II. Importkeramik aus dem Friedhof U in Abydos (Umm el-Qaab) und die Beziehungen Ägyptens zu Vorderasien im 4. Jahrtausend v. Chr., *Archäologische Veröffentlichungen* 92, Mainz.

Hartung, U., 2008, Ein Fragment eines verzierten Dolchgriffs aus dem Friedhof U in Abydos (Umm el-Qaab), in Engel, E.-V., Müller, V., Hartung, U., (eds.), *Zeichen aus dem Sand. Streiflichter aus Ägyptens Geschichte zu Ehren von Günter Dreyer, MENES Studien zur Kultur und Spache der ägyptischen Frühzeit und des Alten Reiches* 5, Wiesbaden, 183-194.

Hartung, U., 2016, Chronological Aspects of the Development of Funerary Equipment in Cemetery U at Abydos (Umm el-Qaab), in Adams, M.D. (ed), 2016, *Egypt at its Origins, Orientalia Lovanensia Analecta* 252, Leuven, 271-298.

Hikade, T., 1996, Die lithischen Kleinfunde, in Dreyer, G., Engel, E.-M., Hartung, U., Hikade, T., Köhler, E.C., Pumpenmeier, F., 1996, *Umm el-Qaab, Nachuntersuchungen im frühzeitlichen Königsfriedhof 7./8. Vorbericht, Mitteilungen des Deutschen Archäologischen Instituts Abteilung Kairo* 52, 34-39.

Kelterborn, P., 1984, Towards Replicating Egyptian Predynastic Flint Knives, *Journal of Archaeological Science* 11, 433-453.

Midant-Reynes, B., 1987, Contribution a L'Etude De La Sociéte Prédynastique: Le Cas Du Couteau "Ripple-Flake", *Studien zur Altägyptischen Kultur* 14, 185-224.

Naville, E., 1914, *The Cemeteries of Abydos Part I: 1909-10. The mixed cemetery and Umm el-Ga'ab*, London.

Needler, W., 1984, *Predynastic and Archaic Egypt in the Brooklyn Museum*, New York.

Petrie, W.M.F., 1896, *Naqada and Ballas 1895*, London.

Scharff, A., 1926, *Die Archaeologischen Ergebnisse des Vorgeschichtlichen Gräberfelds von Abusir el-Meleq*, Leipzig.

Schmidt, K., 1993, Comments to the lithic industry of the Buto-Maadi culture in Lower Egypt, in: Krzyżaniak, L., Kobusiewicz, M., Alexander, J. (eds.), 1993, *Environmental changes and human culture in the Nile Basin and Northern Africa until the 2nd millennium BC, Studies in African Archaeology* 4, Poznan, 267-277.

Wittaker, J.C., 1994, *Flintknapping: making and understanding stone tools*, Austin.

About the author

Dr Thomas Hikade is currently an honorary associate with the Department of Archaeology at the University of Sydney. He is a specialist in Egyptian stone-tools technology. He has taught at the University of Sydney, University of British Columbia in Vancouver, Brown University in Rhode Island, and the University of Trier in Germany. He worked on excavations throughout Egypt, in Jordan and Germany. In 2000 he worked on the stone tools at Tell Ibrahim Awad.

Forgotten excavations, part IV

The first excavation season at Kufur Nigm/Ezbet el-Tell (1961)

Aiman Ashmawy Ali

Introduction

The Forgotten Excavations project aims to publish the mostly unpublished early excavations carried out by the SCA (former EAO) in order to save the data from being lost. One of these early excavations was conducted at the site of Kufur Nigm. It is situated about 2 km north of the village of Kufur Nigm, in the Ibrahimia district, Sharquia Province, about 30 km north of the city of Zagazig. The site is also called Ezbet el-Tell as it is situated south-east of the village with the same name. The site includes three *tells,* separated by modern canals and roads, that were once one large *tell.* The largest of the three *tells* is situated to the south of Ezbet el-Tell. It measures 7 *feddans* and is about 50-150 cm above the present surface. The second *tell* is situated south-east of the first, measures 4 *feddans* and is 2.5-4 m above the present surface. The third *tell* is the smallest of the three: it measures 0.7 *feddans.*

In ancient times the site was a large *gezira* situated to the west of the Tanitic branch of the Nile, which follows the modern Bahr Mous canal. Traces of the *gezira* sand were still visible in the early twentieth century, as it is documented in the modern map of Egypt.[1]

History of excavation at the site

The *tell* was first investigated by archaeologists in 1960, when the Agricultural Committee asked the archaeological authorities to map the area and safeguard its antiquities so that the land could be used for agriculture as laid out in agricultural reforms. In 1961 the Egyptian Antiquities Organisation (EAO) carried out excavations at the site. The work led to the discovery of an early-dynastic cemetery, a rare find in the Delta. As a result of this find the EAO decided to exclude the area from the agricultural reclamation project and retained it under its supervision. In 1978 the EAO excavated at the site for another season under the direction of Hamdey Yussef. Four additional seasons under the auspices of Zagazig University were carried out between 1984 and 1990 under the direction of

1 Map of Egypt (scale 1/2500), sheet 894/672.0, Kufur Nigm and El-Khdaria surveyed 1953.

in: Bercken, B.J.L. van den, 2021. *Egyptian Delta archaeology. Short studies in honour of Willem van Haarlem*, Leiden: Sidestone Press, pp. 47-54.

Dr Mohamed Ibrahim Bakr. The excavations mainly concentrated on the large *tell* south of the village of Ezbet el-Tell, where over 134 tombs were discovered dating back to the early-dynastic period. Among the copious grave goods of different materials were a pottery jar and a sherd, both inscribed with the name of King Narmer. The results of these excavations were published in several short articles; over 180 objects were exhibited in Zagazig University.[2] This paper focuses on the 1961 season, the results of which were not published.

The first excavation season at Kufur Nigm

After the Agricultural Committee asked the archaeological authorities to map the land and safeguard its antiquities, the EAO appointed Dr Iskander Asaad as director of the work.[3] The mission lasted five weeks: from 6 May until 12 June 1961. As there was pressure from the agricultural authorities to see results, Asaad used long excavation trenches to cover the whole area in a short period (fig. 1b). In the northern *tell* 16 trenches were dug which are still visible today (length 75 m x width 1.7 m x depth 1.6 m). The work was supervised by Rashid Noear and Naguib Farag, who visited the site twice and made short reports about the work. Asaad discovered over seventy tombs, mostly from the archaic period but also some later burials. Gabriele Wenzel and Mohamed Bakr incorrectly attributed three hundred tombs discovered by Mohamed Abd el-Haq Ragap at Bani Amer (north of Tell Basta) to the contemporaneous site of Kufur Nigm, where in the first two seasons over seventy tombs were found.[4] The tombs at the site can be divided into the following types:

- type I: pit tombs;
- type II: pit tombs lined with mud bricks;
- type III: burials in pottery coffins with vaulted lid;
- type IV: burials in pottery coffins with vaulted lid lined with mud bricks;
- type V: mud-brick tombs with attached storeroom;
- type VI: burials in pottery jars;
- type VII: big *mastabas* with a storeroom.

Most of the tombs were not completely excavated. The excavator documented only the part of the tomb within the trench and did not uncover the whole tomb. The big *mastabas* (type VII) are characterised by rows of pottery jars that extend for more than 12 m (fig. 1a). The building in which these jars were stored must therefore have been of equal size or larger, perhaps comparable to the ones in Saqqara.[5]

The large-scale use of pottery coffins in the cemetery is noteworthy. In the first season 20 pottery coffins were discovered besides the ones found by Zagazig university, which makes it the largest number discovered on one site in the northern Delta. They are rectangular in shape while the average size is length 100 cm x width 55 cm x height 30 cm, with the thickness of their wall 3-4 cm. One of the coffins had a pottery mark. Examples of

---

2 Bakr 1988, 49-52; Bakr 1994, 9-15; Wenzel/Bakr 2010, 5-10.

3 At that time the land was the property of El-Walada Basha, the mother of the Khedive.

4 Wenzel/Bakr 2010, 5.

5 Quibell 1923, pl. XVI.1.

Fig. 1A Pottery jars arranged in two long rows, excavation of the 1961 season; 1B long excavation trench with pottery coffins; 1C mud-brick tomb with pottery coffin and attached storeroom; 1D later burials in an extended position (image A-D SCA scientific archive).

Fig. 2 Different pottery types from the 1961 season at Kufur Nigm (image: colour photos by the author, black-and-white photos SCA scientific archive).

pottery coffins in Lower Egypt can be found at Tell el-Murra[6], Kafr Hassan Dawood[7], Tell el-Farkha[8] and Turah.[9]

In the early-dynastic tombs the deceased was buried in a contracted or semi-contracted position on his or her left side with the head north and the face to the east, while in the later burials the deceased was buried on his or her back, in an extended position with the hands beside the body (fig. 1d).

During the first season numerous small finds of high quality were made; some of them were chosen to be exhibited in Herriat Raznah Museum until it was closed in 2006. These are now re-exhibited in the Tell Basta site museum. The rest of the finds were packed in boxes and moved to the basement of the Cairo Museum, from which they were brought back to the archaeological storehouse at Tell el-Yahudia in 2010 to be checked by an archaeological committee. They are now kept in the archaeological storehouse at Tell Basta.

Among the pottery finds are (fig. 2): tall storage jars with tapering bodies (also called wine jars); tall storage jars with tapering bodies and a narrow flat base, some without decoration and others with a rope band decoration, typical of the early-dynastic period;[10] tall jars with an ovoid body and a narrow flat base; jars with an ovoid body and a pointed base; cylindrical jars imitating alabaster vessels (examples of these are also known from

6 Jucha, Bąk-pryc and Czarnowicz 2014, 144 fig. 4 right and fig. 5; Jucha, Bąk-pryc and Czarnowicz 2015, fig. 3-5 and fig. 9.

7 Hassan et al. 2003, 40 fig. 5.

8 Chłodnicki and Ciałowicz, 2018a, 117 fig. 54.

9 Junker 1912, 22, Pl.19-24.

10 Hassan et al. 2015, Fig.9; El-Baghdadi 2003, 144, Fig. 4a-b, Van Den Brink 1988, 79, pl.14-15.

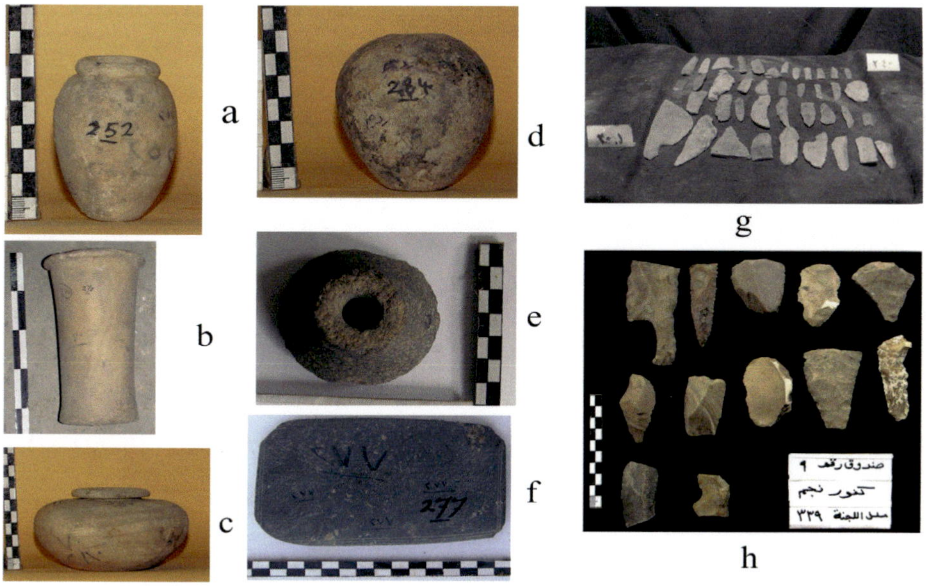

Fig. 3 Stone tools and objects from the 1961 season at Kufur Nigm (image: colour photos by the author).

other sites in the Delta, such as Tell Ibrahim Awad[11] and Tell el-Farkha[12]); one bread mould made of coarse Nile clay with pot marks (parallels are found at Tell el-Fara'in,[13] Tell Abu el-Hayat, Tell el-Akhdar[14] and Tell el-Murra[15]); and one pottery vessel in the shape of a bird (another example of this is found at Tell el-Farkha[16]).

Among the stone objects were (fig. 3): two bracelets made of schist; three palettes of grey stone (greywacke) of which two were rectangular in form and decorated with engraved parallel lines, while the third is oval in shape and without decoration (parallels are found at Minshat Abu Omar and Tell el-Farkha[17]); one piriform limestone mace head and one disc-shaped granite mace head (parallels are found at Tell Ibrahim Awad and Tell el-Farkha[18]); plates made of alabaster, schist and diorite, and boat-shaped grinding stones made from sandstone. A quartzite vase drill with traces of use may point to a local manufacture of stone objects.

Flint tools found in the 1961 season include (fig. 3): over 20 bifacial knives with and without handles; sickle blades; scrapers and borers; and flakes that may indicate a local lithic industry.

The over 55 pot marks found on sherds and complete jars are worth noting (fig. 4). The majority were incised pre-firing and parallels can be found at other Delta sites, such

11 Van Haarlem 1997, 145ff.
12 Chłodnicki et al. 2004, fig. 15-16; Jucha 2008, Fig. 5-9.
13 Hartung et al. 2007, fig. 5, fig. 12.4; Hartung, Engel and Hartmann 2012, 106 Fig. 19.
14 Jucha, Błaszczyk, Buszek, Pryc, 2013 114, 117, Fig. 7, Fig. 8.1.
15 Małecka-Drozd, Kazimierczak 2018, 64, Fig. 3.1-4, Fig. 9-12.
16 Sobas 2012, 194-195, fig. 7.7.
17 Kroeper 1988, Fig. 129-131, 154-155; Kroeper 1996, 81-84, fig.2-8; Chłodnicki 2012, 32, Fig. 22.
18 Van Haarlem 2009, 92-93, Pl. 16-17; Ciałowicz 2012, 176, Fig. 24; Kroeper 1988, fig .46.

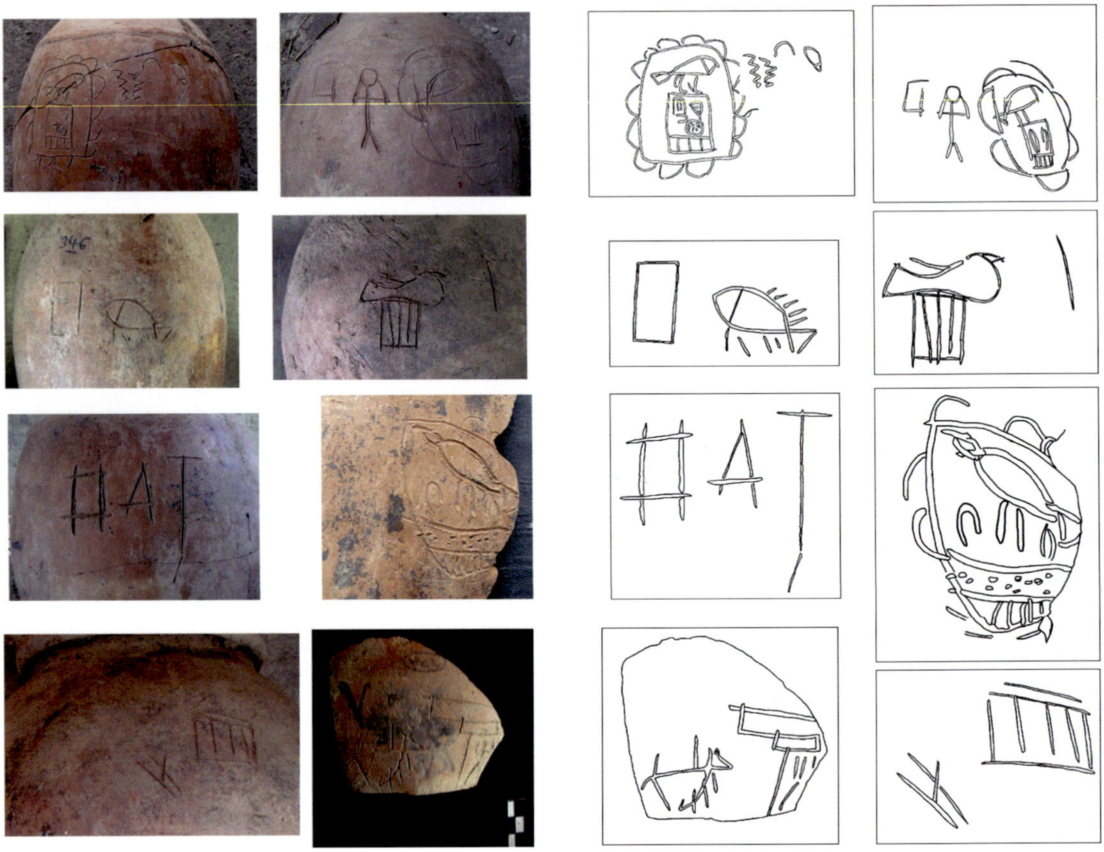

Fig. 4 Pot marks from the 1961 season at Kufur Nigm (image by the author).

as Tell Ibrahim Awad, Kafr Hassan Dawood, Minshat Abu Omar and Minshat Ezzat.[19] Some are considered rare in the Delta, especially those which show the *serekh* inside a royal domain or a fort or fortified town. Six *serekh* signs were discovered during the 1961 season, including a plain *serekh* and a *serekh* with a royal name. Four of these *serekhs* were represented inside a royal domain belonging to kings from dynasty 0 to the 2nd dynasty, including Ka and Semerkhet. This is rare in Lower Egypt, though parallels have been found at Minshat Abu Omar,[20] Helwan[21] and Abydos.[22] Some of these signs on pottery appear in the Delta for the first time, for example the standing man with raised arms, the only parallel for which comes from Abydos. Petrie interpreted the raised arms as a wig.[23]

Further studies of the grave goods from Kufur Nigm will shed more light on the history and culture of the Delta and its relations with Upper Egypt in this early period of Egyptian history.

19 Van Haarlem 1996, 11-12, fig.2, Pl. 1-2; Tassie et al. 2008, 227; Kroeper 1988, fig. 157, 206, 212; El-Baghdadi 2003, fig. 4.

20 Kroeper 1988, pl. 13.

21 Saad 1951, Pl. LXXI.4.

22 Petrie 1900, Pl. XLIV-XLVI; for *serekh* signs see: Van den Brink 1996; Van den Brink 2001.

23 Petrie 1900, 30, Pl. XLVII.

Bibliography

Bakr, M.I., 1988, The New Excavations at Ezbet et-Tell, Kufr Nigm; The First Season 1984, in Brink, E.C.M., van den (ed.), *Archaeology of the Nile Delta, problems and priorities*, Amsterdam, 49-62.

Bakr, M.I., 1994, Excavations of Kufur Nigm, in Berger, C., Clerc, G., Grimal, N. (eds.), *Hommages à Jean Leclant* 4, Le Caire, 9-17.

Brink, E.C.M. van den, 1988, The Amsterdam University Survey expedition to the north-eastern Nile Delta (1984-1986), in Brink, E.C.M., van den (ed.) *Archaeology of the Nile Delta, problems and priorities*, Amsterdam, 65-114.

Brink, E.C.M. van den, 1996, The incised serekh-signs of Dynasties 0-1, part I: complete vessels, in Spencer, J. (ed.), 1996, *Aspects of early Egypt*, London, 140-158.

Brink, E.C.M. van den, 2001, The pottery-incised serekh-signs of Dynasties 0-1. Part II: fragments and additional complete vessels, *Archéo-Nil* 11, 23-100.

Chłodnicki, M., 2012, Lower Egyptian, Protodynastic and Early Dynastic settlements on the northern part of the Eastern Kom, in Chłodnicki, M., Ciałowicz, K.M., Mączyńska, A. (eds.), *Tell el-Farkha I: excavations 1998-2011*, Poznań-Kraków, 19-34.

Chłodnicki, M., Cialowicz, K.M., 2018a, Polish Excavations at Tell el-Farkha (Ghazala) in the Nile Delta: Preliminary Report 2014 – 2018, *Archeologia* 68, 81-154.

Chłodnicki, M., Ciałowicz, K.M., Abłamowicz, R., Dębowska, J., Małecka-Drozd, N., Kazimierczak, M., 2018b, The Nile Delta settlements during the 3rd Millennium BC. The view from Tell el-Murra, in Ciałowicz, K.M., Czarnowicz, M., Chłodnicki, M. (eds.), 2018, *Eastern Nile Delta at the turn of the 4th Millennium BC*, Kraków, 59-69.

Ciałowicz, K.M., 2012 Protodynastic and Early Dynastic settlement on the Western Kom, in Chłodnicki, M., Ciałowicz, K.M., Mączyńska, A. (eds.), 2012, *Tell el-Farkha I: excavations 1998-2011*, Poznań-Kraków, 163-180.

El-Baghdadi, S.G., 2003, Proto- and Early Dynastic Necropolis of Minshat Ezzat Dakahlia Province, Northeast Delta, *Archéo-Nil* 13, 143-152.

Haarlem, W.M. van, 1996, A tomb of the First Dynasty at Tell Ibrahim Awad, *Oudheidkundige Mededelingen uit het Rijksmuseum van Oudheden* 76, 7-34.

Haarlem, W.M. van, 1997, Imitations in pottery of stone vessels in a protodynastic tomb from Tell Ibrahim Awad, *Archéo-Nil* 7, 145-150.

Haarlem, W.M. van, 2009, Temple Deposits at Tell Ibrahim Awad, Amsterdam.

Hartung, U., Ballet, P., Béguin, F., Bourriau, J., Dixneuf, D., Driesch, A., von den, French, P., Hartmann, R., Herbich, T., Kitagawa, C., Kopp, P., Lecuyot, G., Nenna, M.-D., Schmitt, A., Senol., G., Kaan Senol, A., 2007, Tell el-Fara'in – Buto 9. Vorbericht, *Mitteilungen des Deutschen Archäologischen Instituts, Abteilung Kairo* 63, 69-166.

Hartung, U., Maria, E., Hartmann, R., 2012, Tell el-Fara'in – Buto 11. Vorbericht, *Mitteilungen des Deutschen Archäologischen Instituts, Abteilung Kairo* 68, 83-114.

Hassan, F.A., Tassie, G.J., Tucker, T.L., Rowland, J.M., Wetering, J. van, 2003, Social dynamics at the Late Predynastic to Early Dynastic site of Kafr Hassan Dawood, East Delta, Egypt, *Archéo-Nil* 13, 37-46.

Hassan, F.A., Tassie, G.T., Rehren, T., Wetering, J. van, 2015, Ongoing Investigations at the Predynastic to Early Dynastic site of Kafr Hassan Dawood: Copper, Exchange and Tephra, *Archéo-Nil* 25, 75-90.

Jucha, M.A., Kirkowski, R., Mączyńska, A., 2004, Polish excavations at Tell el-Farkha (Ghazala) in the Nile Delta: Preliminary Report 2002 – 2003, *Archeologia* 55, 47-74.

Jucha, M.A., 2008, Wavy-handled and cylindrical jars in the Nile delta: a view from Tell el-Farkha, *Studies in Ancient Art and Civilization* 12, 63-74.

Jucha, M.A., Błaszczyk, K., Buszek, A., Pryc, G., 2013, Tell el-Murra (Northeastern Nile Delta Survey: season 2010), *Polish Archaeology in the Mediterranean* 22, 105-120.

Jucha, M.A., Bąk-Pryc, G., Czarnowicz, M., 2014, Tell el-Murra (Northeastern Nile Delta Survey: season 2012-2013), *Polish Archaeology in the Mediterranean* 23/1, 141-152.

Jucha, M.A., Bąk-Pryc, G., Czarnowicz, M., 2015, Tell el-Murra (Northeastern Nile Delta survey: season 2011), *Polish Archaeology in the Mediterranean* 24/1, 199-214.

Junker, H., 1912, *Bericht über die Grabungen der Kaiserl. Akademie der Wissenschaften in Wien auf dem Friedhof in Turah: Winter 1909-1910*, Wien

Kroeper, K., 1988, The excavations of the Munich East-Delta Expedition in Minshat Abu Omar, in Brink, E.C.M. van den (ed.), 1988, *Archaeology of the Nile Delta, problems and priorities*, Amsterdam, 11-46.

Kroeper, K., 1996, Minshat Abu Omar: burials with palettes, in Spencer, J. (ed.), *Aspects of early Egypt*, London, 70-92.

Petrie, W.M.F., 1900, *The royal tombs of the First Dynasty*, London.

Quibell, J.E., 1923, *Excavations at Saqqara (1912-1941)*, Cairo.

Saad, Z.Y., 1951, Royal Excavations at Helwan (1945-1947), *Supplément aux Annales du Service des Antiquités de l'Egypte* 14, Le Caire.

Sobas, M., Pottery from the Western Kom, in Chłodnicki, M., Ciałowicz, K.M., Mączyńska, A. (eds.), 2012, *Tell el-Farkha I: excavations 1998-2011*, Poznań-Kraków, 181-197.

Tassie, G.J., Hassan, F.A., Wetering, J. van, Calcoen, B., 2008, Corpus of potmarks from the Protodynastic to Early Dynastic cemetery at Kafr Hassan Dawood, Wadi Tumilat, East Delta, Egypt, in Midant-Reynes, B. Tristant, Y. (eds.), *Egypt at its origins 2: proceedings of the international conference "Origin of the State. Predynastic and Early Dynastic Egypt"*, Leuven, 203-235.

Wenzel, G., Bakr, M.I., 2010, Kufur Nigm: An Early Dynastic Cemetery in the Nile Delta, in Bakr, M.I., Brandl, H., Kalloniatis, F. (eds.), 2010, *Egyptian Antiquities from Kufur Nigm and Bubastis*, Berlin, 5-14.

About the author

Aiman Ashmawy Ali is head of Egyptian antiquities sector SCA/Cairo Egypt. He carried out excavations at different sites in Egypt, including: the cemetery of the third pyramid at Giza, Tell el-Kuᶜ, Tell el-Maskhuta and Tell Daphne in the Ismailia governorate, Souk el-Khamis, Matarya (Ain Shams), Tell el-Yahudia Qalubia, Tukh el-Karamus, Tell Ghrir Markaz Kafer Saker, Tell Basta, El-Swa Markaz Abu-Hammad in Sharquia, Nabta Playa in the Western Desert, Baharia Oasis, Tell Hebua (northern Sinai), Taposiris Magna (west of Alexandria). He also joined foreign missions working in Egypt, including the Egyptian-Polish mission at Tell Atrib 'Benha', the German mission at Qantir/Piramesse, the Austrian mission at Tell el-Dab'a/Avaris, the French mission at Tanis 'San el-Hagar', the Dutch mission at Tell Ibrahim Awad and the Egyptian-German mission at Tell Basta.

Buto: towards a further investigation of the Old Kingdom?

Clara Jeuthe and Rita Hartmann

Introduction

Buto (Tell el-Fara'in) is one of only a few known large settlement hills in the western Delta (Kafr el-Sheikh Province) and it has been part of the research agenda of the German Archaeological Institute since 1983.[1] Today, the site still covers an area of roughly 1 km^2. Its ruins rise above the surrounding land by almost 20 m. But only the remains of the late occupancy phases in Buto (in particular the Ptolemaic until the early Islamic periods) are visible above the surface. By contrast, the oldest evidence of human habitation is below the groundwater level and can only be reached with the help of pumps; hence it is investigated in small trenches only. Nonetheless, the long-term research – in particular the combination of different prospection methods, including geomagnetic and drill surveys as well as limited test trenches on the one hand and on the other the large-scale excavations by Ulrich Hartung between 1998 and 2018 – result in an overview of the general development of the site, covering a timespan of more than 3500 years.[2]

From huts to palace

The main excavation (the so-called E trenches) covering an area of more than 2000 m^2 was located at the western edge of the *kôm*, next to the modern village of Sechmawy. This resulted in a full stratigraphical sequence from the fourth millennium BC until the end of the Early Dynastic period (around 2650 BC), witnessing the development from simple huts in the earliest settlement layers towards a palatial residence. This structure presumably controlled (the organisation of) local agriculture and the production of luxury goods such as flint knives, which is also attested. Further evidence such as seal impressions associated

1 Further research in Buto is carried out by the Ministry of Antiquities (directed by Hossam Ghoneim), the team of the University Paris Nanterre/IFAO (directed by Pascale Ballet) as well as by the Department of Geography of Frankfurt University (directed by Jürgen Wunderlich).

2 As an introduction to the DAI work in Buto with further biographical references, see Hartung et al. 2019, Hartung 2018, Hartung 2014, Hartung et al. 2016, Jeuthe/Hartung 2019.

in: Bercken, B.J.L. van den, 2021. *Egyptian Delta archaeology. Short studies in honour of Willem van Haarlem*, Leiden: Sidestone Press, pp. 55-60.

with state officials[3] also emphasises the importance of Buto during this period, its role as a major regional centre and presumably as a royal residence.

The Old Kingdom at Buto

While Early Old Kingdom pottery was found during the excavations, remains of buildings were sparse. This might be due to the massive levelling and resettling activities during the Late Period. The Old Kingdom is well attested by the results of the drilling survey. They indicate that the site developed into a large settlement area from predynastic times onwards and stretched for almost 1 km along the western *kôm* edge and along an ancient waterway. This settlement is still well attested in the late Old Kingdom. There is no further evidence, however, of human activity after the Old Kingdom and before the Third Intermediate Period around 800 BC, when reoccupation started. Although not fully understood at the moment, there must have been a major change in the ancient landscape leading up to that development. This is supported by drastic shifts of the waterways evidenced by geomorphological investigations by the University of Frankfurt.[4]

So while there is a solid understanding of the development of the site before the Old Kingdom and there are insights into the political and economic position of Buto in the Predynastic and Early Dynastic Periods, we still lack knowledge of what happened afterwards. The palatial structure was demolished in the second half of the 2nd dynasty with traces of only little resettlement activity afterwards preserved in the excavated areas.[5] In contrast, the results of the geomagnetic survey as well as the core drill survey hint at the

Fig. 1 View towards the northern edge of Buto, image DAI.

3 See also Engel in Hartung et al. 2012, 109-113.
4 See Wunderlich/Gineau 2014/2015 with further references.
5 See also Ziermann 2002, 484-497.

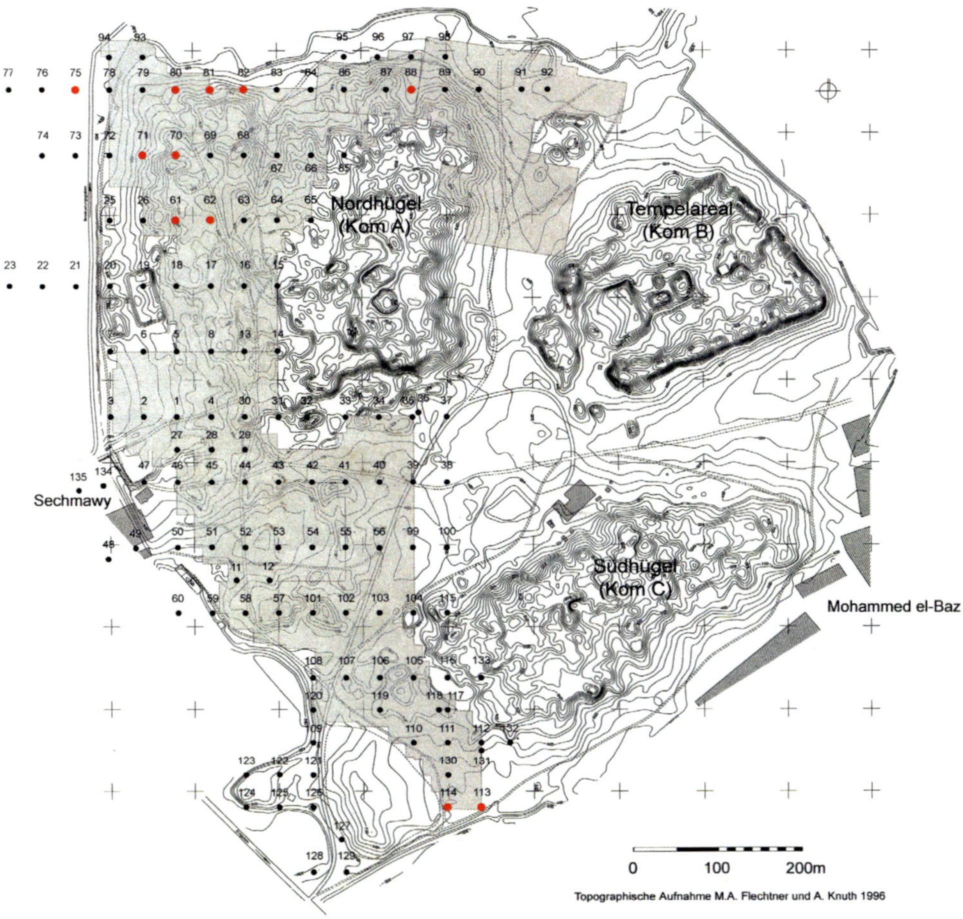

Fig. 2 Drill survey plan, with the red dots indicating the positions of the late Old Kingdom deposits, plan by U. Hartung and R. Hartmann, based on a plan by M. A. Flechtner and A. Knuth.

existence of massive structures possibly dating from the Old Kingdom at the north-western edge of the *kôm*. There, the first excavations took place in a limited excavation area (the so-called J trenches) between 2006 and 2008. Based on associated deposits the brickwork that was found likely dated from the Old Kingdom. The major structures visible in the geomagnetic map, however, turned out to be tomb constructions, likely from the Saite Period, as well as burials from the Third Intermediate Period (eighth-sixth century BC).[6] They clearly disturb the walls and deposits with a presumed Old Kingdom date, but have the same orientation. Conceivably, the older walls were visible when the area was reused as an elite cemetery after the hiatus. It remains unclear, however – although not unlikely – whether the area had a specific ritual or funeral character in the early phases of occupancy.[7]

---

6 Hartung et al. 2009, 87-93; Hartung et al. 2007, 71, 96-98.

7 Hartung et al. 2009, 93.

Nevertheless, the north-western edge of Buto (fig. 1) appears to be one of the few possibilities to investigate the Old Kingdom habitation in more detail, as in other areas it was buried under massive later deposits and structures, eroded, or probably lies underneath the modern settlement.[8] Hence new excavation work was scheduled to start at the northern edge in spring 2020, but had to be postponed due to the Covid-19 pandemic. Based on the results of the excavations so far we hope to gain more insights into the possible changes, but also into ongoing traditions from the late Early Dynastic Period onwards. This will also give us an understanding of the impact of the political and social reorganisation in the beginning of the Old Kingdom. Other research questions concern the ancient settlement topography; Buto's position within local and regional networks of exchange; and the nature of the decline and abandonment of Buto in the late Old Kingdom, as indicated by simpler architecture and material culture.

Ceramic analysis

Although the fieldwork was postponed, the first results from the analyses of earlier ceramic finds by Rita Hartmann can be presented. As a preparation for the planned fieldwork, this study started in 2019 with a re-evaluation and full study of the ceramic finds coming from the core drilling.[9] These finds date from the late 2nd to the 6th dynasty. Their distribution shows clear concentrations with a chronological pattern. From the southern and the north-western areas of the *kôm*, for example, came mainly pottery

Fig. 3 Samples of Old Kingdom pottery from the drill core, image R. Hartmann.

8 See Ziermann 1992.

9 See Hartmann in press; cf. Hartmann et al. forthcoming.

typical of the late Old Kingdom, while the early Old Kingdom might be better attested in the area in between those concentrations (fig. 2). This first impression needs to be verified by future research as the dating of the small sherds from the core drills is difficult (fig. 3). Nonetheless, if we combine these results with the Old Kingdom pottery coming from the excavated E trenches, a continuous habitation in the central part of the western *kôm* until the early 5th dynasty at the latest is conceivable. Moreover, these finds can be functionally linked with food production and supply and may therefore indicate simple settlement activities. By contrast, most of the pottery from the excavated J trenches dates from the late 4th to mid-6th dynasty, while evidence of later occupancy is scarce. Furthermore, earlier activities are not well attested either. Among the finds are not only ceramics that are well known in settlement contexts but also vases attested in ritual contexts. Yet these are without a clear distribution.[10]

Thus the first results of the analysis of the ceramics point to a shift of the settlement area from the centre towards the north of the western *kôm* and on the other hand may indicate different functional zones. With these promising first results, we hope to be able to test the preliminary hypotheses in more detail with future fieldwork at the north-western edge of Buto and present a more differentiated understanding of the ancient settlement during the Old Kingdom.

Bibliography

Hartmann R., (in press), The Old Kingdom settlement at Tell el-Fara'in/Buto – an archaeological and ceramic evaluation, *Mitteilungen des Deutschen Archäologischen Instituts, Abteilung Kairo* 77.

Hartmann, R., Jeuthe, C., Konert, S.-M., (forthcoming), Die Arbeiten des DAI zu Buto (Ägypten) in den Jahren 2019 u. 2020. Aktuelle Arbeiten und Ausblicke, *Deutsches Archäologisches Institut Berlin, E-Forschungsberichte*.

Hartung, U., 2018, Gouvernorat Kafr esch-Scheich, Ägypten: Tell el Faraʿin (Buto) im Nildelta. Die Arbeiten der Jahre 2017 und 2018, *Deutsches Archäologisches Institut Berlin, E-Forschungsberichte*, 2018, Fasc. 2, 39-43, https://publications.dainst.org/journals/index.php/efb/article/view/2148

Hartung, U., 2014, Die Siedlungsgeschichte des Fundplatzes Buto (Tell el Fara'in), *Deutsches Archäologisches Institut Berlin, E-Forschungsberichte*, 2014, Fasc. 3, 9-13, https://publications.dainst.org/journals/index.php/efb/article/download/1712/4628

Hartung, U., Hartmann, R., Kindermann, K., Linseele, V., Ownby, M.F., Riemer, H., 2019 (2020), Buto, Ägypten Tell el-Fara'in – Buto, 13. Vorbericht, *Mitteilungen des Deutschen Archäologischen Instituts, Abteilung Kairo* 75, 147-196.

Hartung, U., Hartmann , R., Kindermann, K., Riemer, H., Stähle, W., 2016 (2017), Tell el-Fara'in – Buto. 12. Vorbericht, *Mitteilungen des Deutschen Archäologischen Instituts, Abteilung Kairo* 72, 73-126.

Hartung, U., Hartmann, R., Engel, E.-M., 2012, Tell el-Fara'in – Buto. 11. Vorbericht, *Mitteilungen des Deutschen Archäologischen Instituts, Abteilung Kairo* 68, 83-114.

Hartung, U., Ballet, P., Effland, A., French, P., Hartmann, R., Herbich, T., Hoffmann, H., Hower, E., Tilmann, A., Kitagawa, C., Kopp, P., Kreibig, W., Lecuyot, G., Lösch, S., Marouard, G., Nerlich, A., Pithon, M., Zink, A., 2009, Tell el Fara'in – Buto. 10. Vor-

10 Cf. Hartmann in press.

bericht, *Mitteilungen des Deutschen Archäologischen Instituts, Abteilung Kairo* 65, 83-190.

Hartung, U., Ballet, P., Béguin, F., Bourriau, J., Dixneuf, D., Driesch, A. von den, French, P., Hartmann, R., Herbich, T., Kitagawa, C., Kopp, P., Lecuyot, G., Nenna, M.-D., Schmitt, A., Şenol, G., Şenol, A., 2007, Tell el-Fara'in – Buto. 9. Vorbericht, *Mitteilungen des Deutschen Archäologischen Instituts, Abteilung Kairo* 63, 69-170.

Jeuthe, C., Hartung, U., 2019, Siedlungsarchäologie im Nildelta – Der Hügel von Buto, *Archäologie in Ägypten: Magazin des Deutschen Archäologischen Instituts Kairo* 5, 60.

Wunderlich, J., Ginau, A., 2014/2015, Paläoumweltwandel im Raum Tell el Fara'in/ Buto: Ergebnisse und Perspektiven geoarchäologischer Forschung, *Mitteilungen des Deutschen Archäologischen Instituts, Abteilung Kairo* 70/71, 485-497.

Ziermann, M., 2002, Tell el-Fara'in – Buto. Bericht über die Arbeiten am Gebäudekomplex der Schicht V und die Vorarbeiten auf dem Nordhügel (site A), *Mitteilungen des Deutschen Archäologischen Instituts, Abteilung Kairo* 58, 461-499.

About the authors

Clara Jeuthe has been a senior research fellow at the Deutsches Archäologisches Institut Kairo since 2019 and is in charge of the Buto settlement archaeology project.

Rita Hartmann is a long-term member of the excavation team in Buto and head of the ceramic studies since 2000.

Four notes on Tia and Iurudef

Jacobus van Dijk

Introduction

By some strange coincidence the year 1982 saw not only the excavation of the tombs of Tia and Tia and their devoted assistant Iurudef by the EES-Leiden expedition to the New Kingdom Necropolis at Saqqara,[1] but also the chance discovery of a complex of chapels at Kafr el-Gebel, just south of Giza, in which the Tias and Iurudef figure prominently.[2] And as it happens 1982 was also the year in which Willem van Haarlem began to participate in fieldwork at Qantir,[3] and the Egyptian Delta has remained his archaeological stamping ground ever since. Since Tia and his family lived in Pi-Ramesse (Qantir) it may be fitting to dedicate the following brief remarks on this *idḥy* to the 'Delta man' Willem.

In 1993 I wrote a chapter on the life and career of the 'overseer of the treasury of the Ramesseum and great overseer of the cattle of Amun-Re king of the gods', Tia, his wife, who was also called Tia and who was a sister of Ramesses II, and his right-hand man Iurudef.[4] The present notes are intended as an update and partial correction of this publication.

Tia in Thebes

The official Tia was probably appointed by Seti I and was most likely married to Seti's daughter before that king's accession. We know very little about his background and his parents are unknown to us, but like virtually every other official he appears to have begun his working life as a 'royal scribe'. This is the sole title he bears on a stela fragment now in the Oriental Museum of the University of Chicago, where he is shown in the company of a 'scribe of the offering table of the Lord of the Two Lands' called Amenwahsu, paying homage to 'the Osiris king' Seti I and his crown prince Ramessu, soon to become Ramesses II. The provenance of this stela is unknown and in 1993 I suggested it may have

1 Martin 1997.

2 By the late Ahmed M. Moussa, see Martin 1997, 1; *DAIK Rundbrief* June 1983, 25; to be published by Bács/Abd el-Aal, forthcoming.

3 Leclant 1983, 469 n. 42.

4 Van Dijk 1993; reprinted with minor alterations in Van Dijk 1997a.

in: Bercken, B.J.L. van den, 2021. *Egyptian Delta archaeology. Short studies in honour of Willem van Haarlem*, Leiden: Sidestone Press, pp. 61-70.

Fig. 1 Tia with Ramesses II on a block from Deir el-Bahari. Image Jadwiga Iwaszczuk, courtesy Mirosław Barwik, Polish-Egyptian Mission in the temple of Hatshepsut at Deir el-Bahari.

come from Abydos,[5] like the stela of May in Brussels which also shows Seti I and Ramessu and refers explicitly to Seti's Abydos temple.[6] As an alternative one might consider the possibility that it comes from Seti's mortuary temple in Gurnah on the Theban west bank.

Be that as it may, an early Theban relief block depicting Tia has recently come to light on the upper terrace of the temple of Hatshepsut at Deir el-Bahari (fig. 1),[7] where it had been thrown down a Third Intermediate Period tomb shaft. Judging by the chisel marks on its surface the slab, which is 1.30 m wide, had been reused at some stage, perhaps more than once,[8] and it was found shattered into as many as 28 fragments. The relief shows a king in the act of burning incense followed by a fan bearer. The names of both are badly damaged, but enough survives to show that the fan bearer was called Tia; of his titles traces of [*ṯꜣy ḫw*] *ḥr* [*wnmy*] *n* [*nsw*] 'fan bearer on the right of the king'[9] are unmistakable and a single *i* just before his name has been plausibly interpreted as being part of the name of Amun in the title 'overseer of the treasury of the temple of Usermaatre-setepenre in the domain of Amun'. The king must surely be Ramesses II, although his cartouches have disappeared almost completely, except clear traces of two *s* signs (O 34) at the end of the nomen. These are enough to show that the King's name was written in its early form *Rꜥ-ms-s*(*w*)[10] rather than the form *Rꜥ-ms-sw* (with M 23) found exclusively in Tia's Saqqara tomb and at Kafr el-Gebel. This in turn agrees well with the suggestion that Tia was involved with the Ramesseum quite early on; in fact he was probably its first

5 It was purchased from Maurice Nahman in Cairo in 1919, cf. Teeter 2003a, 56–7 and 128, where 'Abydos (?)' is suggested. At any rate it does not come from Saqqara, as stated by Brand 2000, 151 (3.39) and 317, who was probably led astray by the inclusion of the fragment in the publication of the Saqqara tomb (Martin 1997, 47–8 [333], Pl. 98).

6 Brussels E. 5300, from Garstang's excavations at Abydos (1906–1909); Brand 2000, 187, 317, figs. 138 and 143.

7 Barwik 2007. I am very grateful to Mirosław Barwik for sending me some excellent colour photographs and allowing me to reproduce one of them here.

8 Barwick 2007, 67 n. 3 suggests it was reused in the kitchen of the Coptic monastery at Deir el-Bahari.

9 See for this title Van Dijk 1993, 95; Van Dijk 1997a, 54.

10 See also Staring 2014–2015, 68.

'overseer of the treasury'.[11] A stamped brick with Tia's name and title of 'chief treasurer' found (reused?) in the area of the mortuary temple of Ramesses IV must originally have come from the Ramesseum.[12] The block from Deir el-Bahari is only 9.3 cm thick, suggesting that it was part of a stone revetment mounted against a brick wall rather than part of a solid stone temple wall. It, too, most likely originated from the Ramesseum, especially since column fragments from that temple have been found reused in the Coptic monastery at Deir el-Bahari as well.[13] One wonders whether Tia may not have had a mortuary chapel within the precinct of the Ramesseum, comparable to that of the Theban mayor Paser at Medinet Habu.[14]

Tia in Pi-Ramesse

That Tia had a house in the great Delta residence of Pi-Ramesse has long been suspected on account of some of his and his wife's titles. The princess Tia in particular is frequently called 'songstress of Amun of Great-of-Victories', a common designation of Pi-Ramesse, both in the Saqqara tomb and in the Kafr el-Gebel chapel.[15] Her husband was steward (*imy-r pr*) as well as high priest (*ḥm-nṯr tpy*) of Amun-of-Ramesses and was also attached to the cult of 'Ramesses-in-the-Sacred-Bark' (*Rꜥ-ms-sw m wiꜣ*), both of which are probably to be linked with Pi-Ramesse.[16] Proof of the Tias' presence at Pi-Ramesse came with the discovery of a column fragment found during the survey of Tell el-Dab'a carried out by Josef Dorner in the early 1980s. It was found near Tell Abu el-Shaf'ei 'lying in an irrigation canal near the bridge over the Bahr Faqous'.[17] The fragment (fig. 2) is inscribed with a single vertical line reading '[... may he/she[18] give m]e joyfulness while being favoured in the King's house, for the Ka of the hereditary prince and count, the royal scribe and great overseer of the cattle of Amun-Re king of the gods, Tia, justified'. Being favoured (or praised) by the king is of course commonplace among high officials,[19] but Tia's reference to the King's house (*pr nsw*) is interesting in the light of two other inscriptions. On a fragment of the wooden outer coffin of Tia from his Saqqara tomb he is called 'one favoured by his god (i.e. the king) when he was (still) a child (*ḥsy n nṯr=f iw=f m nḫnw*)'.[20] A miniature stela of Tia in the Louvre[21] calls him 'the royal scribe, educated by His Majesty (*sbꜣ.n ḥm=f*), raised by the Lord of the Two Lands while (still) in the egg (*sḫpr.n nb tꜣwy m swḥt*), the overseer of the treasury of the temple of Usermaatre-setepenre in the domain of Amun, the

11 For the successive stages of Tia's career see now also Staring 2014–2015, 60–62, 64, 68–69.

12 Van Dijk 1993, 98; Van Dijk 1997a, 55; Martin 1997, 48 [334].

13 Barwik 1990–1991.

14 Schott 1959. For this and other private mortuary chapels at Medinet Habu see Hölscher 1951, 22–5. Note that on the block from Deir el-Bahari Tia's name is followed by *mꜣꜥ-ḫrw ḥr imntt*.

15 Van Dijk 1993, 92; Van Dijk 1997a, 52–53; Abd el-Aal 2009, Pl. 3b.

16 Van Dijk 1993, 96–97; Van Dijk 1997a, 55.

17 Information kindly supplied by Manfred Bietak. I am most grateful to both Prof. Bietak and Edgar Pusch for their efforts to locate the column in their files and for their generous permission to publish a line drawing of it here. The present circumstances unfortunately do not allow access to the documentation of the stone monuments from the site in the Austrian Institute in Cairo or the photographic archive of the expedition.

18 A god or goddess, or perhaps more likely the royal Ka, who is frequently invoked in formulae on domestic architecture.

19 Guksch 1994, 39–45.

20 Raven/Vugts 2011, 173–174 (291a).

21 Louvre E. 7717; Habachi 1969, 45 (7), Pl. 3a; Martin 1997, Pl. 165.

overseer of the cattle of Amun, Tia, justified'. Such phrases came in vogue as part of the ideology of the Amarna Period[22] and are rarely found afterwards. 'Being in the egg' is almost exclusively used for the king himself, not for a private individual.[23] These epithets suggest that Tia was raised at the royal court from early childhood and that he was not of a humble background, as has sometimes been suggested – which would explain why he was able to marry a sister of Ramesses II, albeit long before the latter became king. It is even conceivable that Tia was a distant relative of the Ramesside royal family himself and that he, too, originated from the eastern Delta.

Tia was not the only official with a house in Pi-Ramesse who was buried in the Memphite necropolis. A systematic search for such cases cannot be undertaken here, and much of the Ramesside material excavated in the area of Tell el-Dab'a and Qantir is still unpublished, but among these state officials are the overseer of cattle of the Ramesseum Paraemheb[24] and the chief lector priest and royal envoy Tjuneroy, famous for the Saqqara king-list.[25] The vizier Parahotep is so far attested in Pi-Ramesse only with a stela, but it is likely that he had a house there since he originated from this city.[26]

The King's sister Tia

That Tia's wife was a sister of Ramesses II has almost universally been accepted; after all she explicitly calls herself *snt nsw špst Tiꜣ* 'the King's noble sister Tia' (or perhaps 'the King's sister, the Lady Tia') everywhere in the Saqqara tomb and in the Kafr el-Gebel chapels. A different opinion was expressed by Eva Althoff,[27] who wrote that Tia was probably no more than a distant relative of the King: a cousin or a niece perhaps, or even just a lady from the harem[28] who had been given in marriage to a loyal official. Her main argument is that Tia nowhere calls herself a king's daughter, which she considers to be inconceivable if Tia had been a daughter of Seti I. Surely, however, the title 'King's noble sister' refers to the reigning

Fig. 2 Inscription on a column fragment from Tell el-Dab'a. Image J. Goischke, courtesy Manfred Bietak and Edgar Pusch.

22 Guksch 1994, 31–33, 108–114.

23 It is conspicuously absent from the corpus collected by Guksch 1994. The *Belegstellen* to *Wb.* IV 73, 10 only list a single non-royal example, *Urk.* II 65, 17, which dates from the early Ptolemaic period.

24 Saqqara: PM III^2/2, 771; Staring 2014–2015, 67; Pi-Ramesse: Habachi 2001, 41, 54, 205 (Cat. 84), Pl. 31A.

25 Saqqara: PM III^2/2, 666; Pi-Ramesse: Habachi 1954, 498–499, Pl. 27; Habachi 2001, 41, 54, 56, 193 (Cat. 61), Pl. 21B.

26 Saqqara: PM III^2/2, 665–666; Pi-Ramesse: Habachi 2001, 56 with n. 132. The southern vizier Paser also had a house in Pi-Ramesse (Habachi 2001, 52, 56, 186 (Cat. 52), Pl. 18A); he is the owner of TT 106, but curiously two of his canopic jars appear to have been found at Saqqara, see PM III^2/2, 771; Donahue 1988, 111.

27 Althoff 2004, 37–40.

28 *Špst* as a term designating (former or actual) harem ladies is chiefly known from the Old Kingdom, see *Wb.* IV 450, 1. A New Kingdom example cited in the *Wb.* (IV 450, 2) is termed 'ungewöhnlich' there. In Ramesside times the word *špst* is regularly used for queens and princesses, for instance for the royal ladies buried in the Valley of the Queens which is called *tꜣ st-nfrw (nt) špsw(t)*, where the kings' mothers and noble wives (*ḥmwt šps(wt)* have their tombs, see *KRI* VI 579, 5–7. In Pap. Leiden I 350 vs 2 Isetnofret, a daughter of Merenptah (before he became king), is called *špst* (cf. Janssen 1961, 26). In the 'Tale of the Two

king, Ramesses II, who is omnipresent in the decoration and inscriptions of the Saqqara tomb. This is the reason why the tomb has been called a 'royal monument', not so much because of the presence of the princess Tia: the tomb is explicitly designated as a temple of Osiris built by Ramesses II[29] in which this king is the main officiant. Large-scale cartouches of Ramesses II are present in the pylon gateway of this 'temple-tomb' and elsewhere, and a frieze composed with the nomen and prenomen of the King runs along the top of the pylon and the forecourt, perhaps also that of the peristyle court and beyond. Such friezes are known from many temples of Ramesses II in Egypt and Nubia[30] but not from private tombs. That Tia's wife plays a subordinate role in the tomb reliefs is not at all unusual, it is 'a pattern of decoration typical of a man's tomb in which his wife was also included'.[31]

The high stature of the lady Tia within the royal family is also confirmed by several monuments which show her in the company of Queen Tuia (or Tuy), the mother of Ramesses II and undoubtedly her own mother, particularly on reliefs from Kafr el-Gebel.[32] That she and her husband thus participated in 'the ancestor cult of the Ramesside clan'[33] (including Seti I, Queen Tuia, and Ramesses II as well as the founder of the 18th dynasty, Ahmose I[34]) makes it very unlikely that she was merely a distant relative or even a harem lady married to a 'commoner'. It is a telling fact that we know very little about the lives and marriages of all but the most prominent of the multitude of Ramesses II's sons and daughters.[35] The lady Tia was clearly an exceptional figure within the early Ramesside family.

The early history of this family has been discussed many times, with the famous 'Stela of Four Hundred Years' as the central piece of evidence. In 1993 I did so as well,[36] and I have little to add to my analysis here, except that I now believe Manfred Bietak was right in suggesting that Tia, wife of Paramessu, changed her name to Satre once her husband had become Ramesses I,[37] or rather, that the name Tia represents a hypochoristicon of the name Satre. In the list of princesses on Ostracon Louvre 666 a daughter of Ramesses II is listed with the double name Satre Tia,[38] showing that the two names can refer to one and the same person. The name of Paramessu's wife on the 'Stela of Four Hundred Years' is to

---

Brothers' Bata's treacherous wife is called *tꜣ špst* 'the noble lady' and on one occasion she is explicitely styled the king's wife (*ḥmt-nsw tꜣ špst*, Pap. D'Orbiney 18, 4). One is also reminded of *tꜣ špst Nhrn*, 'the noble lady of Mitanni', the foreign princess who was given in marriage to the Egyptian pharaoh (probably Thutmose IV), see Van Dijk 1997b, 33–36. Thus in the New Kingdom the term *špst* clearly denotes a lady of elevated rank, not a mere inhabitant of the king's harem.

29 Martin 1997, 39 [123], Pl. 66.

30 Van Dijk 1993, 102–106; Van Dijk 1997a, 57–58.

31 Teeter 2003b, 152–153.

32 Bács 2019, 43; Martin 1997, 46 [330], Pl. 95.

33 Bács 2019, 45.

34 Bács 2008.

35 From Ostracon Louvre 2262 we learn that in Year 42 of Ramesses II Sa-montu, the King's twenty-third son, married one Iryt, the daughter of a Syrian ship's captain called Binʿanat – hardly a prestigious liaison, one would imagine; see Spiegelberg 1894, 64; *KRI* II, 907.

36 Van Dijk 1993, 107–111; Van Dijk 1997a, 60–61.

37 Bietak 1975, 185–186, n. 786. See also Polz 1986, 163.

38 Spiegelberg 1894, 67 (top right); *KRI* II, 922. Note that there are also two princesses called Tuia on this list, one of whom has the second name Nebettawy.

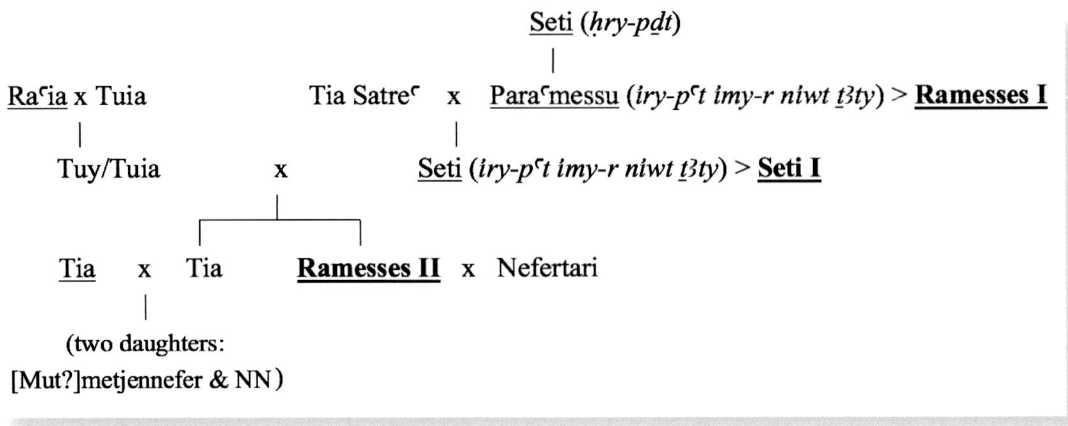

Fig. 3 Genealogy of the early Ramesside royal family.

be read Tia, not Tiu, as is still occasionally stated in error in the literature.[39] This Tia was therefore our Tia's grandmother (fig. 3).[40]

Iurudef and his family

The 'scribe of the treasury' Iurudef obviously played a major role in the life of the Tias, perhaps because the couple do not seem to have had any male offspring. As treasury scribe he was Tia's assistant[41] and as such he appears in several places in the tomb, notably on the ends of the balustrade flanking the shallow ramp leading up to the central offering chapels of the tomb and in the relief depicting the voyage to Abydos.[42] He constructed his own little tomb chapel in the forecourt of Tia's tomb, where he is given the additional title of 'scribe of the divine offerings'. Iurudef also appears in the chapels of Kafr el-Gebel, often in the company of Tia and Tia; here he is not only called 'scribe of the treasury', but also 'overseer of works for his lord (i.e. Tia) in Ro-Setau'[43] and 'overseer of works of Ramessu-in-the-Sacred-Bark',[44] an institution also mentioned in connection with Tia himself.

Very little remains of the superstructure of Iurudef's tomb. His wife was clearly mentioned in it, but nothing beyond 'his "sister" (wife), the songstress [...]'[45] and possibly '[... of A]mun'[46] survives. Of the shabtis retrieved from the burial chambers those of Iurudef call him 'scribe (of the treasury)', but one of them has 'scribe of the divine offerings of all the gods'.[47] Among the other shabtis, four mention a woman (*nbt-pr*) called Akhes

39 Repeated collation under different light circumstances confirms that the bird sign in question is an *ꜣ*, with tail and wings which nearly touch the ground and with a clear square head, and *not* the quail chick *w*; see already Van Dijk 1993, 109 n. 88; Van Dijk 1997a, 60 n. 5.

40 The first sign in the name of Queen Tuy's non-royal mother, tentatively read as the lion *rw* (E 23) before, almost certainly reads *ṯ* (V 13). The *rw* sign is almost always followed by the ideographic stroke (Z 1), not by the phonetic complement *w* (Z 7) as is the case here. The name of Tuy's mother is therefore most probably to be read as Tuia.

41 Van Dijk 1993, 98–101; Van Dijk 1997a, 56–57.

42 Martin 1997, 24 [56, 57], Pl. 36 and 28 [81–83], Pls 47, 154, resp.

43 Martin 1997, Pl. 94 [328a].

44 Martin 1997, Pl. 95 [329].

45 Raven 1991, Pl. 4d; Martin 1997, Pl. 56 [105].

46 Raven 1991, Pl. 4c; Martin 1997, Pl. 56 [104].

47 Raven 1991, Pls 38 and 44 [1].

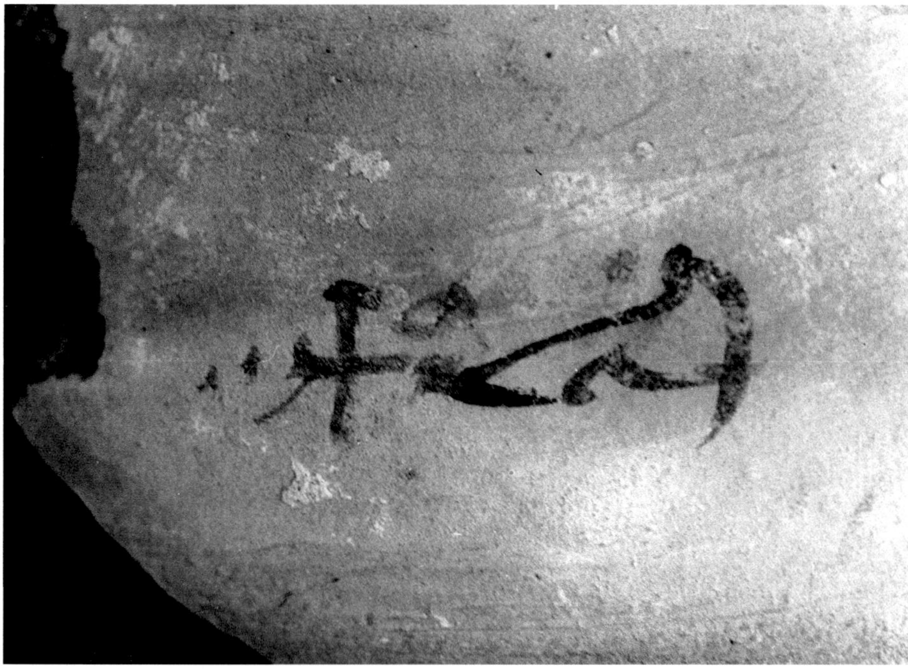

Fig. 4 Hieratic docket on amphora fragment 83-S60 from the tomb of Tia at Saqqara. Image M. Vinkesteijn/Rijksmuseum van Oudheden, Leiden.

who Raven suspected might be Iurudef's wife, and a 'scribe of the treasury Tia', possibly their son.[48] These family connections have since been confirmed by the discovery of two rectangular framed stelae (Nos. 43 and 44) in the Kafr el-Gebel complex.[49] On stela No. 43 the Tias are shown worshipping Osiris in the upper register. The offering formulae on the frame are for the benefit of 'the scribe' Iurudef. In the lower register Iurudef, again simply called 'scribe', and his family are depicted. His wife is called the *nbt-pr* Akhes (spelled *ꜣḫ-sw*); she is followed by two daughters, Henutmehyt and the songstress of Amun Bak(et)-mut, and two sons, Tia and Amenemopet, who are both shown on a smaller scale and do not bear any titles. Clearly these two boys were still young when the stela was erected. Stela No. 44 was dedicated by (*ir.n*) Iurudef, who is called 'scribe of the treasury of the domain of Amun(-Re) King of the Gods', 'overseer of works in Ro-Setau' and 'overseer of works of the temple of Ramessu-in-the-Sacred-Bark'. The upper register shows Osiris being worshipped by the 'overseer of the treasury of the Lord of the Two Lands' Amenemopet followed by Iurudef. The lower register is very similar to the one of No. 43, only the six persons are all shown on the same scale. They are Iurudef, his wife Akhes, their two daughters and their sons Tia and Amenemopet who are now both scribes of the treasury. These two sons obviously followed in their father's footsteps. The eldest is named after Iurudef's superior Tia, the second after the Amenemopet shown in the upper register, who

48 Raven 1991, 2. Shabtis of Akhes: Pls 38, 44 [26a-d]; of Tia: Pls 38, 45 [28].

49 Abdel-Aal 2000.

may have been Tia's successor as 'chief of the treasury of the Lord of the Two Lands'.[50] Judging by the presence of the shabti the son Tia was probably buried in the family tomb at Saqqara, while his brother Amenemopet may be tentatively identified with the scribe of the treasury of the Ramesseum Amenemopet who was the owner of TT 374.

The confirmation of the name of Iurudef's wife Akhes enables us to solve the 'mystery' of a hieratic docket on an amphora found in a pottery deposit immediately south of the staircase between the tombs of Horemheb and Tia. Since some of the sherds from this 'staircase cache' joined sherds found in the burial chambers of Tia and Tia, there can be little doubt that this amphora was cleared out of Tia's tomb at some stage.[51] It is inscribed with the phrase *ꜣḫ sw* followed by two dots (fig. 4). In the publication I suggested this was to be translated as 'He/it is beneficial (?)',[52] mainly because two other amphorae from this deposit were inscribed with water dockets and served a cultic purpose. As an alternative I proposed to read it as a proper name, referring to the feminine name *ꜣḫ.s(y)* listed by Ranke.[53]

This option is clearly to be preferred now, and the two dots are to be interpreted as the seated female determinative. This means that Iurudef's wife donated an amphora (containing water?) to the funeral goods of her husband's master, a modest but touching tribute to the man after whom she named her eldest son.

Bibliography

Abdel-Aal, S., 2000, A Memphite family from the Ramesside Period, *Mitteilungen des Deutschen Archäologischen Instituts, Abteilung Kairo* 56, 1–4.

Abd el-Aal, S.S., 2009, Some blocks belonging to the Tias from Kafr el-Gebel, in Rössler-Köhler, U., Tawfik, T. (eds.), 2009, Die ihr vorbeigehen werdet… Wenn Gräber, Tempel und Statuen sprechen. Gedenkschrift für Prof. Dr. Sayed Tawfik Ahmed, *Sonderschriften des Deutschen Archäologischen Instituts, Abteilung Kairo* 16, Berlin/New York, 1–4.

Althoff, E., 2004, Familienbande? Tia – die vermeinte Schwester von Ramses II., *Antike Welt* 35: 1, 37–40.

Aston, D., 1984, § 6. – Saqqara (Excavations of the Egypt Exploration Society and Leiden Museum), *Bulletin du Liaison du Groupe International d'Etude de la Céramique Egyptienne* 9, 13–14.

Bács, T.A., 2008, Ahmose at Rosetau: A curious early Ramesside attestation, in Szabó, Á., Vargyas, P. (eds.), 2008, *Cultus deorum. Studia religionum ad historiam*, Vol. I: *De oriente antiquo et regione Danuvii praehistorica. In memoriam István Tóth*, Budapest, 111–22.

Bács, T.A., 2019, Early Ramesside royalty at Rosetau, *Saqqara Newsletter* 17, 32–45.

50 The only 'overseer of the treasury of the Lord of the Two Lands' Amenemopet known to me is the man who was also 'overseer of the granaries of Upper and Lower Egypt' and who was nicknamed Panehsy (Louvre C 65, l. 5), but this man lived during the last decades of the 18th dynasty, see Bohleke 2002. Could the Amenemopet on Iurudef's stela likewise be an alter ego of the Panehsy who succeeded Tia as chief treasurer (cf. Van Dijk 1993, 106; 1997, 59; Staring 2014–2015, 68)? See also the case of the owner of the Late New Kingdom Book of the Dead Berlin No. 2 (Naville's manuscript *Be*) who is called both Panehsy and *Ỉpy*, a hypochoristicon of *Ỉmn-m-ipt*, see Sethe 1907–1908, 92.

51 Aston 1984, 13–14; Aston, in Martin 1997, 96.

52 Van Dijk, in Martin 1997, 72 (Cat. 53), Pl. 106.

53 Ranke 1935, 3: 9.

Bács, T.A., Abd el-Aal, S., forthcoming, *The Ramesside monuments of Kafr el-Gabal. A contribution to the history of the Giza area in the New Kingdom.*

Barwik, M., 1990–1991, Fragments of columns from the Ramesseum found at Deir el-Bahri, *Memnonia* 1, 19–24.

Barwik, M., 2007, Overseer of the Treasury Tia at Deir el-Bahari, *Memnonia* 18, 67–70.

Bietak, M., 1975, *Tell el-Dab'a II. Der Fundort im Rahmen einer archäologisch-geographischen Untersuchung über das ägyptische Ostdelta, Untersuchungen der Zweigstelle Kairo des Österreichischen Archäologischen Institutes* 1, Vienna.

Bohleke, B., 2002, Amenemopet Panehsi, direct successor of the chief treasurer Maya, *Journal of the American Research Center in Egypt* 39, 157–172.

Brand, P.J., 2000, *The Monuments of Seti I. Epigraphic, Historical and Art Historical Analysis, Probleme der Ägyptologie* 16, Leiden etc.

Donahue, V.A., 1974, The vizier Paser, *Journal of Egyptian Archaeology* 74, 103–123.

Dijk, J. van, 1993, The King's brother-in-law Tia, in Dijk, J. van, 1993, *The New Kingdom necropolis of Memphis: Historical and iconographical studies*, Groningen, 84–112.

Dijk, J. van, 1997a, The family and career of Tia, in Martin, G.T., 1997, *The Tomb of Tia and Tia: A royal monument of the Ramesside Period in the Memphite necropolis, EES Excavation Memoir* 58, London, 49–62.

Dijk, J. van, 1997b. The Noble Lady of Mitanni and other royal favourites of the Eighteenth Dynasty, in Dijk, J. van (ed.), *Essays in honour of Herman te Velde, Egyptological Memoirs* 1, Groningen, 33–46.

Guksch, H., 1994, *Königsdienst. Zur Selbstdarstellung der Beamten in der 18. Dynastie, Studien zur Archäologie und Geschichte Altägyptens* 11, Heidelberg.

Habachi, L., 1954, Khatâ'na-Qantîr: Importance, *Annales du Service des Antiquités de l'Égypte* 52, 443–559.

Habachi, L., 1969, La reine Touy, femme de Séthi I, et ses proches parents inconnus, *Revue d'Egyptologie* 21, 27–47.

Habachi, L., 2001, *Tell el-Dab'a I. Tell el-Dab'a and Qantîr. The site and its connection with Avaris and Piramesse, Untersuchungen der Zweigstelle Kairo des Österreichischen Archäologischen Institutes* 2, Vienna.

Hölscher, U., 1951, *The Excavation of Medinet Habu, Vol. IV: The Mortuary Temple of Ramses III, Part ii, Oriental Institute Publications* 55, Chicago.

Janssen, J.J., 1961, Two Ancient Egyptian ship's logs. Papyrus Leiden I 350 verso and Papyrus Turin 2008+2016, *Oudheidkundige Mededelingen uit het Rijksmuseum van Oudheden te Leiden Supplement* 42, Leiden.

Leclant, J., 1983, Fouilles et travaux en Egypte et au Soudan, 1981–1982, *Orientalia* 52, 461–542.

Martin, G.T., 1997, *The Tomb of Tia and Tia: A royal monument of the Ramesside Period in the Memphite necropolis, EES Excavation Memoir* 58, London.

Polz, D., 1986, Die Särge des (Pa-)Ramessu, *Mitteilungen des Deutschen Archäologischen Instituts, Abteilung Kairo* 42, 145–166.

Ranke, H., 1935, *Die ägyptischen Personennamen, I: Verzeichniss der Namen*, Glückstadt.

Raven, M.J., 1991, *The Tomb of Iurudef: A Memphite official in the reign of Ramesses II, EES Excavation Memoir* 57, Leiden/London.

Raven, M.J., Vugts, M., 2011, New evidence on the tomb of Tia, in Raven, M.J., Verschoor, V., Vugts, M., Walsem, R. van, 2011, *The Memphite tomb of Horemheb, Commander in chief of Tutankhamun, Vol. V: The forecourt and the area south of the tomb with some notes on the tomb of Tia, Papers on Archaeology of the Leiden Museum of Antiquities* 6, Turnhout, 153–189.

Schott, S., 1957, *Wall scenes from the mortuary chapel of the mayor Paser at Medinet Habu. Studies in Ancient Oriental Civilizations* 30, Chicago.

Sethe, K., 1907–1908, Über einige Kurznamen des neuen Reiches, *Zeitschrift für Ägyptische Sprache und Altertumskunde* 44, 87–92.

Spiegelberg, W., 1894, Ostraca hiératiques du Louvre, *Recueil de Travaux relatifs à la philologie et à l'archéologie égyptiennes et assyriennes* 16, 64-67.

Staring, N., 2014–15, The personnel of the Theban Ramesseum in the Memphite necropolis, *Journal of the Ancient Near Eastern Society 'Ex Oriente Lux'* 45, 51–92.

Teeter, E., 2003a, *Ancient Egypt: Treasures from the collection of the Oriental Institute, University of Chicago. Oriental Institute Museum Publications* 23, Chicago.

Teeter, E., 2003b, Review of Martin, G.T., 1997, The Tomb of Tia and Tia: A royal monument of the Ramesside Period in the Memphite necropolis, EES Excavation Memoir 58, London, *Journal of Near Eastern Studies* 62, 151–153.

About the author

Dr Jacobus van Dijk was associate professor of Egyptology at the University of Groningen, the Netherlands. He worked for many years as philologist/epigrapher with the EES-Leiden mission at Saqqara, the Cambridge Expedition to the Valley of the Kings, and the Brooklyn Museum Expedition to the Precinct of Mut at South Karnak.

Worked mollusc remains from Qantir/ Piramesse

Chiori Kitagawa

Introduction

Qantir, ancient Piramesse, is located in the eastern Delta, *c.*100 km north-east of Cairo (fig. 1). The excavations and on-site study seasons have been carried out since 1980, led by Edgar B. Pusch (1980-2015, Roemer-Pelizaeus Museum Hildesheim) and Henning Franzmeier (from 2015 onward, Roemer-Pelizaeus Museum Hildesheim/Humboldt-Universität zu Berlin/Università di Bologna). The project has shed light on various aspects of human activities at the residence of Ramesses II (19th dynasty; thirteenth century BC). One of the most notable results was the revealing of ancient production activities, including technology associated with workshops for a wide variety of materials. Some of these production activities were discovered at the excavation area Q I (fig. 2), for example the bronze foundry in the northern half of Q I and affiliated workshops for metal, wood, stone and animal remains in the south: strata B/3a, b.[1] The foundry was later turned into a chariot practice yard, which was substantiated not only by the finds of chariot parts made of stone and bronze but also by hoof prints of horses in the corresponding stratum B/2.[2] The southern workshop area remained in use with changes to its layout and was used to produce and supply arms for the garrison of the ancient capital.[3] Located east of Q I, Q IV was excavated in the 1990s, where layers relating to small workshops (strata Bc/d/e) and the royal stables of the chariotry from the later strata (Bb/c) were discovered.[4] Other excavation areas, Q V (excavated from 1999 to 2000) and Q VII (excavated from 2000 to 2004), were also investigated. Architectural remains of the workshop rooms and

1 Pusch 1990; Pusch 1999; Pusch/Rehren 2007, 21-30; Pusch/Becker 2017, 46-54. As to glass production: 'Südlich der "Gasse", die dem Exerzierhof parallel verläuft, befinden sich Werkstätten, in denen Glas sehr wohl hätte hergestellt und verarbeitet werden können' (Pusch/Rehren 2007, 25). Although no definitive architectural evidence (facilities) for producing glass have been found within the excavated area at Q I, it is very likely that glass was also produced, as they operated high-temperature technology for bronze.

2 Pusch/Becker 2017, 45-59 Tab. 01.

3 Pusch/Becker 2017, 45-59.

4 Pusch/Rehren 2007, 21-40; Pusch/Becker 2017, 45-68 Tab. 03. At Q IV there was a large quantity of glass-related finds, though no architectural structure was found that could provide evidence of glass processing at Q IV (as at Q I, see footnote 1).

in: Bercken, B.J.L. van den, 2021. *Egyptian Delta archaeology. Short studies in honour of Willem van Haarlem*, Leiden: Sidestone Press, pp. 71-77.

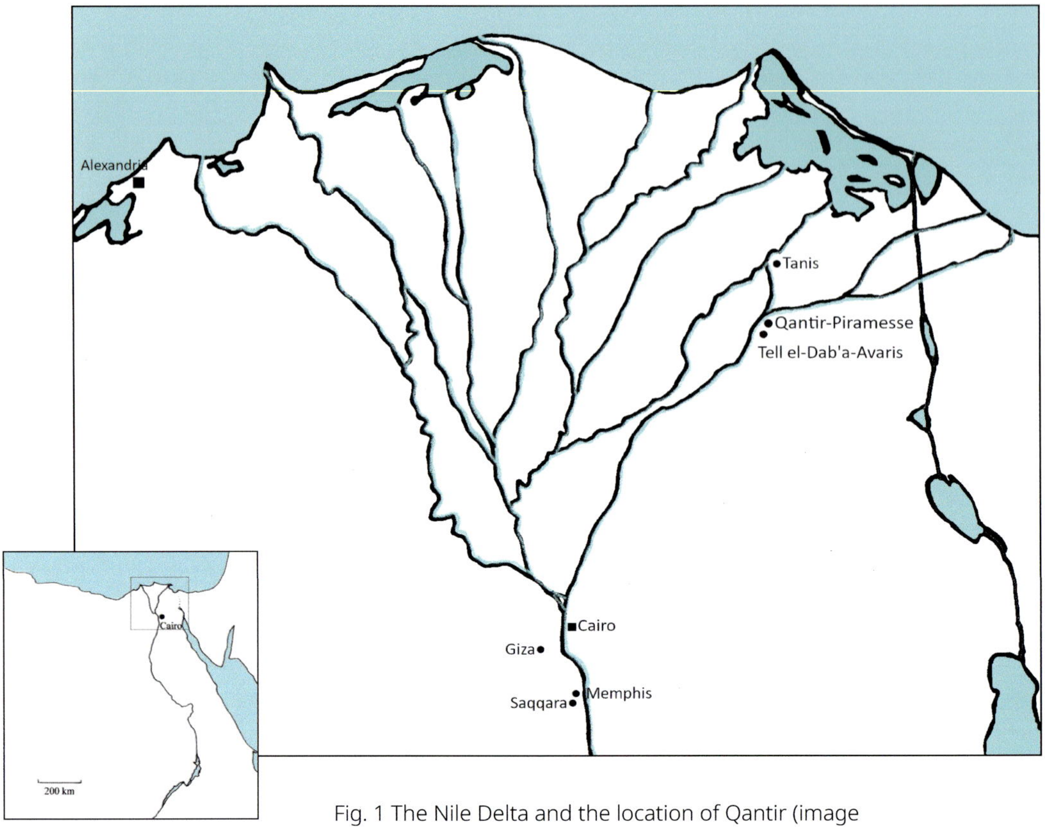

Fig. 1 The Nile Delta and the location of Qantir (image Chiori Kitagawa).

storerooms from the 19th dynasty, spacious buildings from the 19th and 20th dynasties, refuse pits and the watercourse (canal) from the Persian period were unearthed at Q V.[5] In Q VII a fragment of a cuneiform tablet was found outside Building A (a building with a columned hall), which indicates foreign diplomacy between Ramesses II and the Hittites.[6]

Worked mollusc remains from Qantir: taxa and distribution within the site

In Qantir animal remains from a variety of taxa were discovered, which included a number of worked faunal remains of mammals (N=383), molluscs (N=80) and unidentified specimens (N=2).[7] Most of the worked molluscs were found at Q IV, which accounted for *c.*76% (N=61 out of 80 worked molluscs: fig. 3).[8] It is worth noting that a large part of the worked osteofaunal remains of mammals were found at Q I (N=343 out of 383, *c.*90%), which was different from the location where most of the worked molluscs were excavated (Q IV).[9]

5 Pusch/Rehren 2007, 41-44; Pusch/Becker 2017, 76-80.

6 Pusch/Becker 2017, 94-115.

7 Prell/Kitagawa 2020, 43 Tab. 1; Kitagawa forthcoming Tab. 4; Kitagawa in preparation.

8 Prell/Kitagawa 2020, 43 Tab. 1; Kitagawa forthcoming; Kitagawa in preparation.

9 Prell/Kitagawa 2020, 41-43; Kitagawa in preparation.

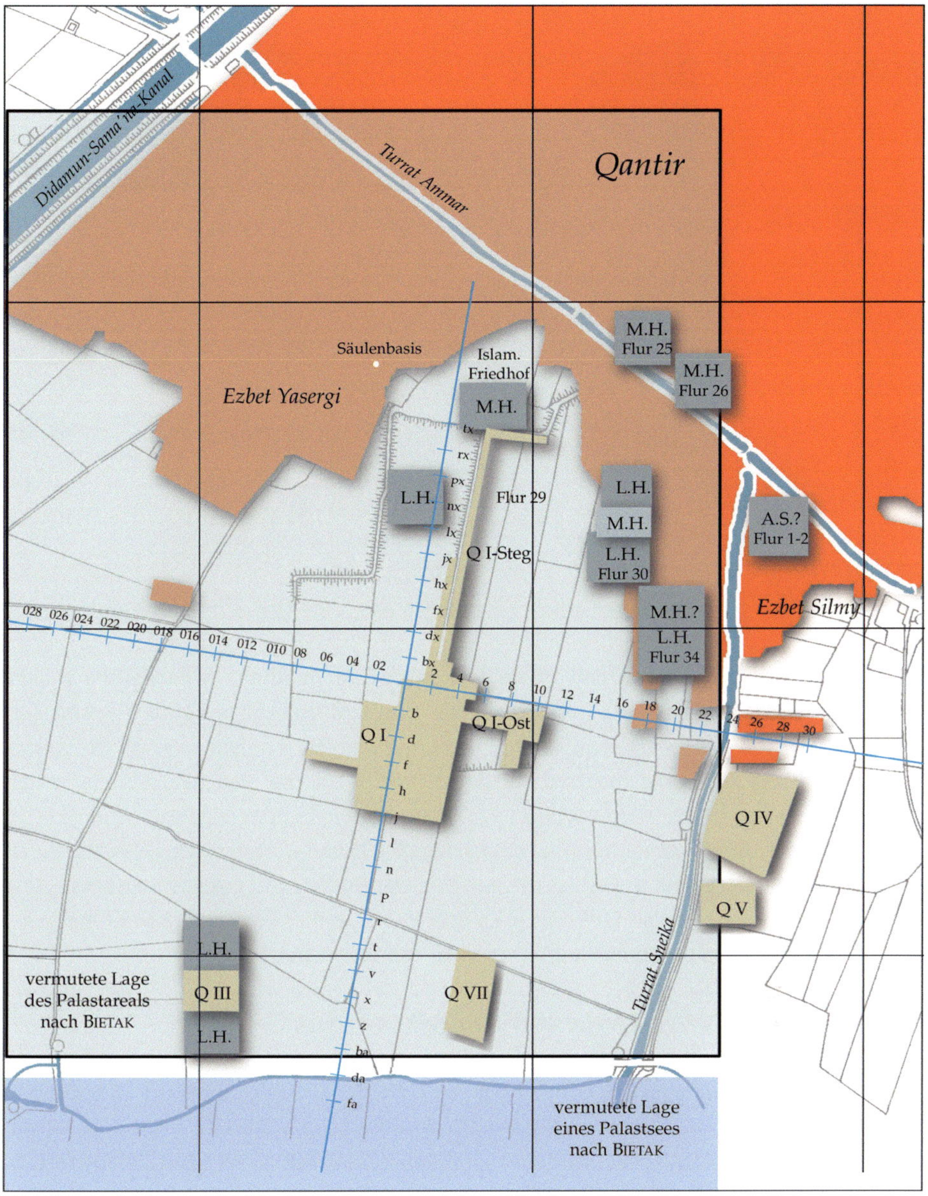

Fig. 2 Map of Qantir south, showing the excavation areas Q I, Q III, Q IV and Q VII and those by M. Hamza (M.H.), A. A. Salam (A.S.) and L. Habachi (L.H.) (after Pusch/Becker 2017, Abb. 033). Each mark on the vertical and horizontal axes indicates 20 m.

Originally the worked molluscs would have been remains of those acquired for food, those acquired for the sole purpose of processing, or those from natural remains. Land snails, freshwater molluscs inhabiting the Nile, its tributaries and lakes, and marine molluscs from the Red Sea and the Mediterranean were included in the malacofaunal assemblages (with and without traces of artificial processing) of Qantir. Among the 80 modified molluscs, marine molluscs were found more frequently than freshwater ones

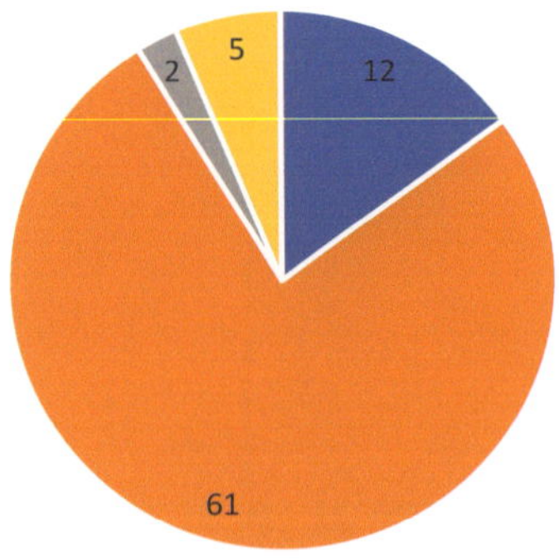

Fig. 3 The number of worked molluscs retrieved per excavation area in Qantir (total N=80) (modified after Kitagawa forthcoming, fig. 7).

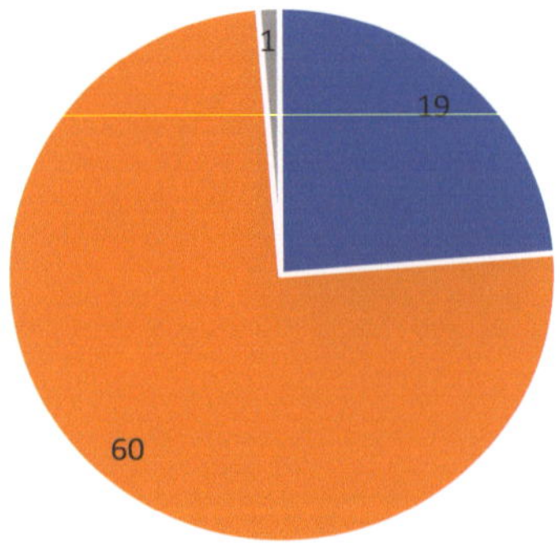

Fig. 4 The number and the habitat of worked molluscs from Qantir (total N=80).

(fig. 4).[10] There were in total (N=) 19 worked freshwater molluscs (*Chambardia rubens arcuata* and *Mutela dubia nilotica*) among the whole of worked mollusc assemblages. Species from the Mediterranean, among which *Columbella rustica* (N=3), *Nassarius gibbosulus* (N=1) and *Cerastoderma* sp. (N=1), and from the Red Sea, among which *Monetaria moneta* (N=1), *Nerita polita* (N=4), *Ancilla acuminata* (N=1) and *Tridacna* sp. (N=1), were exploited in small numbers. Cowries (N=27) and *Glycymeris* sp. (N=21), which inhabit the Mediterranean as well as the Red Sea, were utilised in greater numbers.[11] One of the most frequently found molluscs in Qantir was *Glycymeris* sp. with holes (openings) in their umbones,[12] so that they could have been used as beads.[13]

Artefact types of the worked molluscs from Qantir

It may be worth pointing out that the modified molluscs clustered more at excavation area Q IV, where living quarters (strata Be/f, 18th/19th dynasties(?), Ramesses II, and again later strata Ba, 20th and 21st dynasties, twelfth-tenth century BC), small workshops (strata Bc/d/e, 19th dynasty, Ramesses II) and the royal stables (strata Bb/c, 19th and 20th dynasties, Sety II-Ramesses III, twelfth century BC) were located.[14]

These molluscs, especially those with worked or used edges (for example used as a scoop or a scraper), might have been used as tools in everyday life, at workshops, or both. It is

10 Kitagawa forthcoming; Kitagawa in preparation.

11 Kitagawa forthcoming, Tab. 4; Kitagawa in preparation.

12 The umbo is the highest part above the hinge of a valve.

13 The cause of holes in *Glycymeris* sp. could be either natural or artificial. In nature, these holes are observed in umbones by abrasion on the seashore due to the weathered surface (Sivan et al. 2006, 144; personal observation) and in valves caused by carnivorous gastropods.

14 Pusch/Rehren 2007, 31-40; Pusch/Becker 2017, 62-68.

Object type	Q I	Q IV	Q V	Q VII	Total
Bead	9	45	-	5	59
Ring	1	-	-	-	1
Scoop	1	6	-	-	7
Scoop/Scraper	-	1	-	-	1
Bivalve with worked edge	-	7	-	-	7
Raw material	-	-	1	-	1
Raw material/Debitage	1	-	-	-	1
Raw material/Unfinished artefact	-	2	-	-	2
Palette?	-	-	1	-	1
Total	**12**	**61**	**2**	**5**	**80**

Fig. 5 Number of object types of worked molluscs found at each excavation area in Qantir (modified after Kitagawa forthcoming, tab. 6).

imaginable that such large bivalves could have been used as handy multi-purpose tools.[15] It cannot be ruled out that big bivalves may also have been used in the care for horses at the royal stables. They could have been used to remove sweat and dirt like the 'sweat scrapers' made of metal or plastic nowadays. Moreover, use as a 'rasp' or an equivalent to a modern 'hoof pick' to clean the underside of hoofs, by using the edge of a valve to scrape out soil and dirt, could also be possible. This is merely a hypothesis, however, as so far only few large bivalves (among the small total number of such objects) were found *in situ*. Most of them were derived from the secondary or tertiary contexts.

Mollusc beads from Qantir represented 59 in total (fig. 5).[16] The most common taxa that were found among the mollusc beads were *Glycymeris* with openings in their umbones and cowries (*Cypraeaidae*) which were sawn dorsally.[17] Nearly half of all worked animal remains (bones and molluscs: N=93) recovered at Q IV were mollusc beads (N=45). It illustrates a different picture from that at excavation area Q I, where in many cases osteofaunal remains were used for implements rather than ornaments. A particularly noteworthy archaeological context at Q I was the multi-functional workshops of the strata B/2-/3, where a variety of raw materials was used for producing artefacts, mostly for the pharaoh's troops.[18] Therefore, many of the worked animal remains from Q I were artefacts that related to armour and parts of chariots, as well as half-finished artefacts and waste after processing them.

15 One of the interesting hypotheses is a possible usage of valves of *Chambardia rubens arcuata* (syn. *Aspatharia (Spathopsis) rubens*) as *strigiles*. A number of these valves, with rims that were neither too sharp nor too blunt, were found at bathrooms in Tell el-Dab'a, a neighbouring site of Qantir (M. Bietak, personal communication, 9 December 2020).

16 Kitagawa forthcoming; Kitagawa in preparation.

17 Kitagawa forthcoming; Kitagawa in preparation.

18 Pusch 1990; Pusch 1999; Pusch/Rehren 2007; Pusch/Becker 2017; Prell 2011; Prell/Kitagawa 2020, 46-48; Kitagawa in preparation.

Concluding remarks

The (temporal-)spatial distribution of worked faunal remains on the site is not even. Inhabitants of Qantir seem to have processed faunal remains in the area of Q I beyond their need for the household.[19] On the other hand, more worked molluscs were unearthed at the area Q IV. They were found not in the production area of Q I but rather in the area where they were in use. In the case of mollusc remains, the waste from the production process of the mollusc beads (for example cowrie) has yet to be found. It is possible that the molluscs were processed outside of the areas excavated so far, and therefore did not come to our attention. In terms of ready-to-use tools, such as large bivalves, only post-use molluscs were encountered.

In Qantir we have one of the best-known and most evident examples of a professional pre-industrialised workshop for osteofaunal remains within a multi-functional economic unit. This was particularly well documented at Q I. These workshops produced a large number of products from various raw materials that were controlled by the government of that period.[20] Parallel to this, it is likely that some types of molluscs were used as ready-to-use tools, which was observed at Q IV.

Acknowledgement

The author is grateful to Willem van Haarlem for an opportunity to take part in the excavation of Tell Ibrahim Awad in 2000. I would like to thank Edgar Pusch and Henning Franzmeier for the permission to study and use the materials and for their invaluable support. Silvia Prell was so kind as to discuss this manuscript with me. Thanks also to Manfred Bietak for sharing his thoughts on the possible mollusc usage in Tell el-Dab'a. The Qantir project was supported by the Deutsche Forschungsgemeinschaft (1980-2010/2011) and the author's research on animal remains by the Deutsche Akademische Austauschdienst (2003-2005) and the Japan Society for the Promotion of Science (2005-2008).

Bibliography

Kitagawa, C., forthcoming, Beyond the Household Activities, *Proceedings of the 5th meeting of the (ICAZ) Worked Bone Research Group Velico Turnovo, Bulgaria 2005.*

Kitagawa, C., in preparation, Environment and human activities in ancient Egypt: with a focus on osteofaunal remains from Qantir (eastern Delta) and Lower Egypt (Ph.D. dissertation).

Prell, S., 2011, Einblicke in die Werkstätten der Residenz. Die Stein- und Metallwerkzeuge des Grabungsplatzes Q I, *FoRa* 8: Gerstenberg, Hildesheim.

Prell, S., Kitagawa, C., 2020, The Bone Workshop of the Armoury from the Chariotry of Ramesses II in Qantir-Piramesse – a Case Study, in Hodgkinson, A.K., Tvetmarken, C.L. (eds.), 2020, *Approaches to the Analysis of Production Activity at Archaeological Sites*, Oxford, 39-49.

Pusch, E.B., 1990, Metallverarbeitende Werkstätten der frühen Ramessidenzeit in Qantir-Piramesse/Nord, Ein Zwischenbericht, *Egypt & Levant* 1, 75-113.

19 Kitagawa forthcoming; Kitagawa in preparation.

20 Pusch/Rehren 2007; Pusch/Becker 2017; Prell 2011; Prell/Kitagawa 2020, 46-48.

Pusch, E.B., 1999, Vorbericht über die Abschlußarbeiten am Grabungsplatz Q IV 1997, *Egypt & Levant* 9, 17-37.

Pusch, E.B., Rehren, T., 2007, Hochtemperatur-Technologie in der Ramses Stadt; Rubinglas für den Pharao, *FoRa* 6, Gestenberg, Hildesheim.

Pusch, E.B., Becker, H., 2017, Fenster in die Vergangenheit. Einblicke in die Struktur der Ramses-Stadt durch magnetische Prospektion und Grabung, *FoRa* 9, Gerstenberg, Hildesheim.

Sivan, D., Potasman, M., Almogi-Labin, A., Bar-Yosef Mayer, D.E., Spanier, E., Boaretto, E., 2006, The Glycymeris query along the coast and shallow shelf of Israel, southeast Mediterranean, *Paleogeography, Paleoclimatology, Paleoecology* 233, 134-148.

About the author

Chiori Kitagawa (Freie Universität Berlin/Nagoya University) is a zooarchaeologist with a special focus on animal remains from (but not limited to) ancient Egypt. She has also worked on faunal remains from Turkey and Germany.

An (un-)usual cooking pot from Qantir/ Piramesse[1]

Henning Franzmeier

Willem van Haarlem worked in Qantir between 1982 and 1984. Even though I met him only much later and in a totally different context, it is a great pleasure to offer this small contribution, which includes a sherd that Willem might have excavated himself in 1984.

Introduction

In his magisterial 1998 publication of the Ramesside pottery from site Q I at Qantir/ Piramesse, David Aston defined a small group of vessels as 'black-slipped' and 'burnished black-slipped'.[2] The vessels in this group are not only unusual for their general appearance, but also for one particular vessel shape: a carinated restricted bowl with lug handles – the only vessel ever republished since.[3] While a reassessment of the bowl by the author in 2019 did not confirm the 'burnishing to a high gloss' of the vessel,[4] both the shape and the surface treatment remain rare. The discovery of a much more complete specimen of such a vessel during the 2016 excavations at Qantir/Piramesse makes it worthwhile to return to this peculiar type.

The vessel FZN 16/0304 from 2016 (fig. 1)

Find-slip-number (FZN): 16/0304

Findspot: site Q VIII; square g/7; NS: *c*.5.00-6.00 m WO *c*.7.00-8.00 m a.s.l.= 3.87 m

Stratum (relative): b

Tertiary position

1 I would like to thank David Aston, Sabine Laemmel, Sara Pizzimenti, and Anke Weber for fruitful discussions and suggestions. Moreover, I am grateful to Matthieu Götz, who supplied me with a considerable part of the literature used for this article. All mistakes of course remain my own.

2 Aston 1998, 352-353, Cat.-No. 1235-1240, FZN 84/0869a+0870,0039; 84/0066a,0126; 86/0463a,0002; 84/0066a, 0124; 87/0119,0001; 84/0082a,0029.

3 Wodzinska 2010, 157, type New Kingdom 209.

4 Aston 1998, 352.

in: Bercken, B.J.L. van den, 2021. *Egyptian Delta archaeology. Short studies in honour of Willem van Haarlem*, Leiden: Sidestone Press, pp. 79-85.

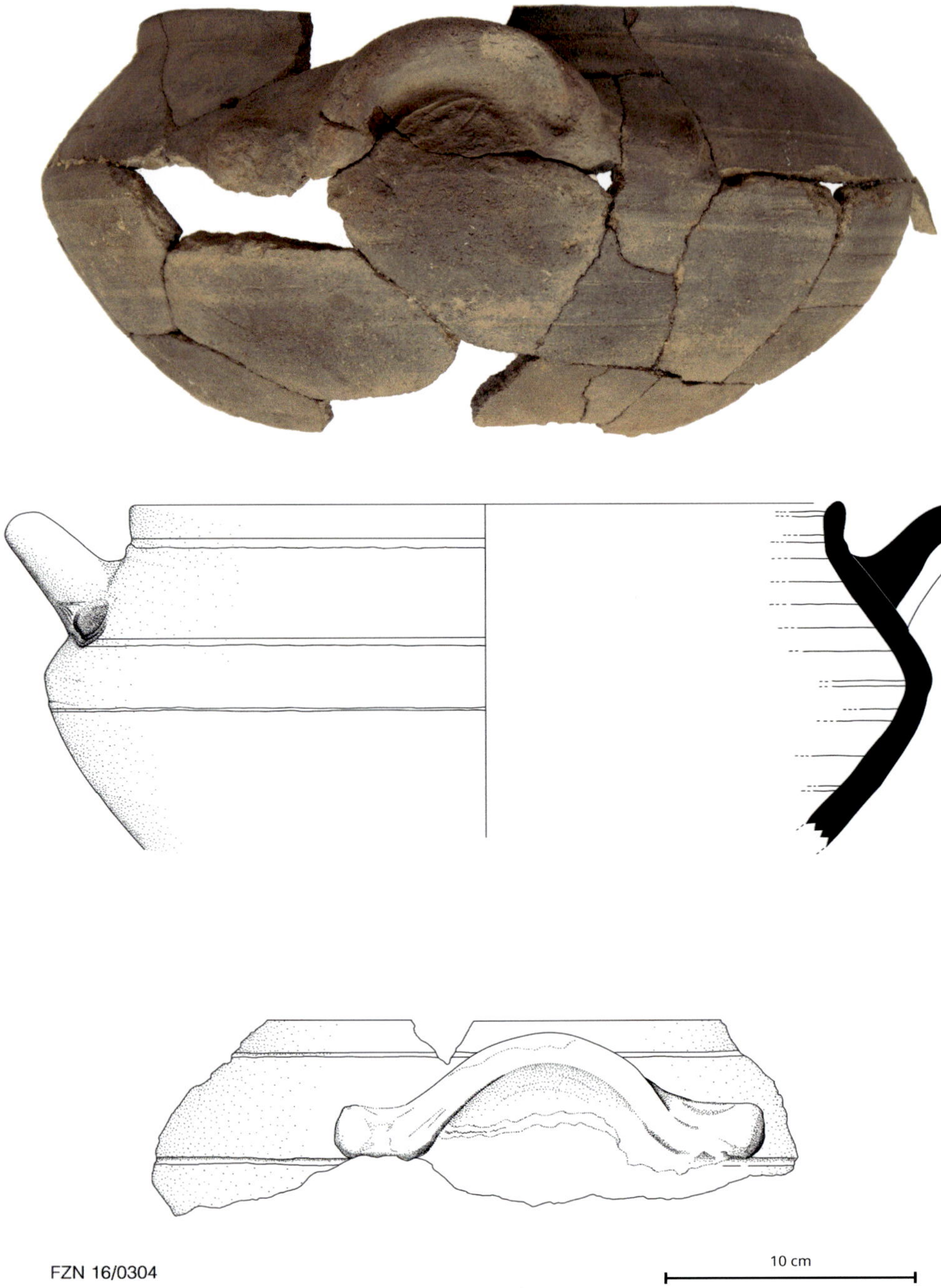

Fig. 1 Vessel Qantir FZN 16/0304 (pencil drawing: Valentina Gasperini; digital version: Barbara Gilli; photo after reconstruction, using Paraloid B 72, by the mission's restorer Meike Büttner; photo: Robert Stetefeld).

Measurements: h. 14.5 + x cm (most likely *c.*18-20 cm) Ø (max.): 34.5 cm Ø rim: 28 cm thickness of wall: 0.8-1.2 cm
Material: fabric I.E.01, surface uncoated and only roughly smoothened. The colour of both the surface and the break is a light to dark grey with the internal colour only slightly different from the outside.
Surface: the surface is only roughly smoothened and does not show any traces of a slip.
Preservation: the vessel was found broken in circa 25 fragments. These were found next to each other and it can be suggested that the vessel was thrown into the pit largely intact and broke during deposition. While most of the body and the rim are present, the base is missing. Extensive surface flaking of the fragments towards the base seems to indicate repeated exposure to heat from below and therefore makes it likely that the vessel was used as a cooking pot. It can be assumed that the base was rounded, but a flat or ring-shaped base cannot be entirely ruled out.
Archaeological context: the vessel was found in a refuse pit [004] in square g/7 in the new site Q VIII.[5] The filling was rich in humus and contained some charcoal and a large number of animal bones and pottery. Most important among this pottery were a small beaker (I.E.0I, red-slipped) with direct rim[6] and larger fragments of dishes of Ramesside types that are very common at Qantir. A domestic or kitchen context seems a likely origin for these materials.

The upper limit of the pit is in the topsoil and thus there is no clear stratigraphic dating. While the ceramic material has not yet been fully analysed, a preliminary analysis by the author points towards the late 19th or early 20th dynasty.

Discussion

The distinctive character of the vessel is based upon the lug handles and the surface colour, which are both unusual for the late New Kingdom at Qantir. Except the fragments published by Aston and the newly discovered almost complete specimen, no close parallels regarding the surface treatment are known to me from Qantir.[7] In contrast, the fabric is by far the most common at Qantir: I.E.01 Nile silt which due to its properties is well-suited for high-temperature applications.[8]

A new analysis of the finds from site Q I by the author did not reveal any trace of a burnished surface on the vessels FZN 84/0066a,0124 and FZN 87/0119,0001[9] (fig. 2). The 'black slip' seems to be the remains of a wash or careful smoothening of the surface with wet hands or a wet cloth, while the colour is the result of the firing process. Based on the analysis of photographs, a parallel for the surface treatment can be found at Deir el-Medina.[10] The new find from Qantir exhibits a much less carefully smoothened surface.

5 For a preliminary report, see Franzmeier in press.

6 Similar in shape to Aston 1998, 132-133, Cat.-No. 275.

7 Personal communication D.A. Aston 29.09.2020. Sites Q IV, Q V, Q VI, and Q VII at Qantir/Piramesse did not yield any comparable fragments (personal communication S. Laemmel 27.09.2020 (Q IV) and personal observation of the author (Q V, Q VI, and Q VII)).

8 Aston et al. 2007, 521-522.

9 The fragment 87/0119,0001 was reconstructed by Aston as a part of a carinated bowl with a high rim (Aston 1998, 353). It cannot be excluded in my opinion that it was also part of a vessel such as FZN 84/0066a,0124 and the newly discovered FZN 16/0304.

10 Nagel 1938, 166, Fig. 138.

FZN 84/0066a,0124

FZN 87/0119,0001

Fig. 2 Photos of FZN 84/0066a,0124 (top) and FZN 87/0119,0001 (bottom) (images: Robert Stetefeld).

5 cm

The general vessel shape can be connected to New Kingdom carinated cooking pots from Qantir[11] and other sites. A restricted bowl of a very similar shape but with horizontal handles comes from Amarna.[12] Rose suggests a slightly later date than the Amarna Period, based on the archaeological context and the red rim band. Parallels for the most characteristic feature – the lug handles – come from Deir el-Medina.[13] Only the surface

11 Aston 1998, 170-171, Cat.-No. 468-473 with further parallels mentioned in the text.

12 Rose 2007, 74, type SE 5.2 and Cat.-No. 261.

13 Nagel 1938, 165-166 and Pl. VI. The closest parallel is the vessel K.2.96.

Fig. 3a Vessel from Deir el-Medina (drawing after Nagel 1938, Pl. VI, K. 2.96).

Fig. 3b Depiction of a large metal cooking vessel from the tomb of Ramesses III (photo: Johannes Kramer, courtesy of The Ramesses III (KV11) Publication and Conservation Project).

treatment of the example from Deir el-Medina with a red and a black zone above the carination differs from the specimens at Qantir (fig. 3a).

Apart from the handles, the vessel type stands in the tradition of earlier Egyptian cooking pots,[14] but it is also very common in non-Egyptian contexts from the Levant –

14 Budka 2016, 294, Fig. 4 (type D).

where cooking pots in general seem to be a much more common find in comparison with Egypt.[15]

While David Aston suggested metal vessels as models that were copied, on the basis of the surface treatment,[16] already in 1938 Nagel connected the vessel from Deir el-Medina with metal prototypes based on their shape and presumed function.[17] To my knowledge there is just one metal parallel known,[18] but comparable metal cooking pots are depicted in various tomb scenes. Both Nagel and Radwan pointed out that probably the best example comes from chamber Ba (south wall) of KV11, the tomb of Ramesses III (fig. 3b), showing obviously much larger but shape-wise similar pots being used to cook meat. The vessels depicted have a metal support to place them over the fire. Another interesting feature of the depicted pot from the tomb of Ramesses III is the black and pink colours used. Somewhat similarly, the cooking pot published by Nagel has a red rim and neck and a black zone around the shoulder, including the handle. Even though never found together, a combination of a metal stand and a metal ring with handles and large ceramic vessels might be a guess.[19] Ceramic vessels of a size matching those represented in KV11 are indeed known from Qantir, although of different types.[20]

As with the bigger pot in the scene in KV11, metal supports might have been used to place the Qantir pot over a fire. More likely it was supported by so called 'fire dogs' which are also known from Qantir, though not from the same context as the recent find.[21]

To sum up, the cooking pots from Qantir and Deir el-Medina can be interpreted as somewhat unusual examples of a very common type of vessel. In their physical properties they follow metal examples to a varying degree. The rare lug handles seem to be an expression of the creativity of Egyptian potters. The general similarity of this type of cooking pot to contemporary foreign examples from the Levant might be taken as one more sign of the international exchange during the Late Bronze Age in the eastern Mediterranean.

---

15 For an overview of the cooking pots of the Late Bronze and Early Iron Age in the Levant and Cyprus see Spagnoli 2010. For carinated cooking pots of a similar type, see Spagnoli 2010, e.g. Plate 8, 55 (Ashdod twelfth century BC) or the many examples from Hazor (Plate 27-28, dating to LB IIB). Many of those also have a very similar surface to the new find from Qantir.

16 Aston 1998, 352.

17 Nagel 1938, 166 with footnote 5. It has to be stated though that only one of the vessels shows traces of fire. Nonetheless, Nagel also suggests use as a cooking pot for the closest parallel K.2.96.

18 Cairo CG 3446. See Radwan 1984, 108 Cat. No. 307.

19 Anke Weber agreed with this idea. Fragments of very large vessels are known from Qantir, even though so far nothing which might potentially match the vessels shown in the tomb of Ramesses III, if the idea regarding the combination of metal stands and ceramic vessels is correct.

20 Unpublished material from site Q IV. The bowls and plates of I.C. Nile Silt reach a diameter of up to 2 metres.

21 For 'fire dogs' in general, see Aston 1989; for the best-preserved examples from Qantir see Aston 1998, 580-581, Cat.-No. 2384. No fragment of a fire dog has so far been found in site Q VIII.

Bibliography

Aston, D. A., 1989, Ancient Egyptian "Fire Dogs" – A New Interpretation, *Mitteilungen des Deutschen Archäologischen Instituts Kairo* 45, 27-32.

Aston, D. A., 1998, Die Keramik des Grabungsplatzes Q I, Forschungen in der Ramses-Stadt 1, Hildesheim.

Aston, D. A., Mommsen, H., Mountjoy, P., Pusch, E. B., Rehren, T., 2007, Die in- und ausländischen Werkstoffe der Grabung Qantir in Wort und Bild, in Pusch, E.B. (ed.), *Die Keramik des Grabungsplatzes* Q I. *Teil* 2. *Schaber – Marken – Scherben. Forschungen in der Ramses-Stadt* 5, Hildesheim, 509-54.

Budka, J., 2016, Egyptian Cooking Pots from the Pharaonic Town of Sai Island, Nubia, *Bulletin de liaison de la céramique égyptienne* 26, 285-295.

Franzmeier, H., in press, Qantir-Pi-Ramesse – Preliminary Report on the 2016 and 2017 seasons (site Q VIII*)*, in Wilson, P. (ed.), *Proceedings of the Delta Survey Workshops 5 and 6 (Alexandria 2017 and Mansoura 2019).*

Nagel, G., 1938, *La céramique du Nouvel Empire à Deir el Médineh, Documents de Fouilles de l'Institut Français D'Archéologie Orientale du Caire* 10, Cairo.

Rose, P., 2007, *The Eighteenth Dynasty Pottery Corpus from Amarna, EES Excavation Memoir* 83, London.

Radwan, A., 1984, *Die Kupfer und Bronzegefäße Ägyptens, Prähistorische Bronzefunde, Abteilung II: Gefäße*, Band 2, München.

Spagnoli, F., 2010, *Cooking Pots as an Indicator of Cultural Relations between Levantine Peoples in Late Bronze and Iron Ages. Origins, diffusion and typological development of cooking ware in Levantine and Cypriot repertoires (14th-7th centuries BC)*, Rome.

Wodzinska, A., 2010, *A Manual of Egyptian Pottery, Volume 3: Second Intermediate Period-Late Period*, Boston.

About the author

Currently Henning Franzmeier is a junior assistant professor at the Alma Mater Studiorum Università di Bologna. Since 2015 he has been the field director of the Qantir/Piramesse Project, run as a cooperation between the Roemer- and Pelizaeus-Museum Hildesheim and the Humboldt-Universität Berlin. He has a PhD in Egyptology from the Freie Universität Berlin and an MA in Egyptology from the Georg-August-Universität Göttingen.

Diversity in the Delta

Egyptian portraits of Persians in the Allard Pierson collection

Geralda Jurriaans-Helle and Laurien de Gelder

Introduction

It is always a pleasure to write a contribution to a *Festschrift*, especially when it is dedicated to a dear – and for one of us life-time – colleague: Dr Willem van Haarlem, curator of the Egyptian Department at the Allard Pierson. For us as coming and going curators of the Near Eastern and Greek Departments of the same museum, however, it is challenging to write about an Egyptian subject for his eyes and amidst a field of esteemed Egyptologists and archaeologists.

Persians in Egypt

Talking about the possibilities we came upon some objects in the Allard Pierson found in Memphis and representing the cultural melting pot that the Delta was from the fifth century BC onwards. In this so-called First Persian Period (525-404/401 BC) a politically unified Egypt was annexed by the Achaemenid Persians, with the great king ruling as a pharaoh on behalf of Auramazdā. Because of its location, Memphis was the cosmopolitan and administrative hub of Egypt and acted as the physical controlling link between the Delta and the rest of Egypt. For Egyptologists and Mediterranean archaeologists alike, Manetho's 27th dynasty (525-404 BC) is not the Egyptian period that is most easily understood. Furthermore there is much debate amongst scholars on the question of to what extent the Achaemenids affected Egyptian material culture, which also makes the archaeological data of this period difficult to date and determine.[1] Laurien recollects that during her collaboration with Willem for the renewed archaeological departments in the museum, there were rather heated arguments on the placement of certain Egyptian artefacts in other rooms than his beloved Egyptian Cabinet. Willem did not object, however, to 'hand over' the two Egyptian artefacts from the Achaemenid period we will discuss in this paper, to be placed in the department on the first millennium BC, *Greeks and Great Powers*.

---

1 Colburn 2020, 1-26. We kindly thank Dr Henry Colburn for sharing his knowledge and thoughts on this object with us.

in: Bercken, B.J.L. van den, 2021. *Egyptian Delta archaeology. Short studies in honour of Willem van Haarlem*, Leiden: Sidestone Press, pp. 87-94.

Fig. 1 Portrait of a Persian king or satrap. Terracotta, Memphis (Egypt), 6th-5th cent. BC, image Allard Pierson, University of Amsterdam, APM07199.

A Persian pharaoh

The starting point of this contribution is a terracotta fragment with the head of a Persian king or satrap in relief (APM07199, fig. 1). It probably came from the excavations Sir William Matthew Flinders Petrie (1853-1942) conducted in Memphis in 1909. The Egyptologist and collector of antiquities Friedrich Wilhelm Freiherr von Bissing (1873-1956), whose legacy Willem has studied extensively, bought it in Cairo from the art dealer Maurice Nahman around 1900 and sold it to Constant Willem Lunsingh Scheurleer (1881-1941) in 1921. In 1934 the fragment became part of the collection of the Allard Pierson Museum.

The fragment (h. 10 cm, w. 8 cm) is made of pinkish-beige clay.[2] Since it is slightly concave, it may have been part of a large vessel turned on the potter's wheel. At the back are shallow ridges and traces of the potter's fingerprints. The fragment shows the head and neck of a man in high relief. A mass of hair falls over his neck and he has a long pointed beard. The smooth hair of the head and beard indicates Egyptian rendering and is often seen in Late Period sculpture. The man is wearing an earring and the high Persian headdress worn by the great kings on the reliefs in Persepolis (fig. 2). He is facing a flat surface that appears to be a column decorated with an incised open lotus flower flanked by two closed lotus buds (*Nymphaea caerulea*). The fragment may be dated to the Late Period, most likely the 27th dynasty (525-404 BC).

---

2 Coll. Von Bissing T 530. Von Bissing 1930, 236 n. 4, pl. 5, fig. 6; Lunsingh Scheurleer 1937, 43, no. 344; Scheurleer 1974, 89 fig. 8a; Van Haarlem/Lunsingh Scheurleer 1986, 65-66 no. 12 (right); Lunsingh Scheurleer 1992, 145 fig. 112; Rehm 2006, 497, Abb. 3; Henkelman 2010, 6-7 fig. 1.

Fig. 2 Portrait of the Great King Darius I, detail of relief on his tomb in Persepolis (after Schmidt 1970, plate 22 B).

Only a few similar portraits have been found, but in all cases provenance and date are uncertain. Colburn suggests these objects to be personal effects and not official royal representations of the great king (on coins, for example). The hat is usually worn by the great king only, while earrings are only seen on courtiers. It is possible that an Egyptian craftsman used a generic Persian costume to present an imperial official or satrap of the great king ruling as pharaoh over Egypt.[3]

The Dutch in the Delta

For Geralda this head from Memphis awoke some memories of Willem and the Delta. In 2001 Geralda was in Cairo for the opening of an exhibition about the Dutch traveller Cornelis de Bruijn (*c.*1652-1727), who visited Egypt in 1681. During the weekend she travelled to Tell Ibrahim Awad in the Delta with the Dutch ambassador to visit the Dutch excavation. There she saw Willem in a role quite different from her quiet fellow curator in the museum: masterfully leading the excavation and receiving the ambassador in grand style, guiding the visitors around the excavation and taking care that a nice object was discovered just at the moment of their arrival.

Cornelis de Bruijn visited not only Cairo and the great pyramids, but also Alexandria, Damietta and Rosetta. He made drawings of the landscape in the Delta (fig. 3) and gives a description of it in his book: 'The Country here appear'd to me, both above and below the Nile, almost like Holland, with good Pastures, and a great many Cattle grazing there, which seem'd to me both a pleasant and surprizing Sight. The River runs with a swift Current, and has on one side a Bank of Sand like the Sounds of Scheveling [Scheveningen].'[4]

---

3 Colburn 2020, 73.

4 De Bruijn 1702, 130, chapter XXXIII. De Bruijn's book was published in the Netherlands in 1698. An English translation was published in 1702. For the sake of Dutch readers we give the original text in the Dutch edition (p. 179, chapter XXXIII): ''t Land doed zich hier, in het op en afvaaren van den *Nyl*, op, bij na even als in *Holland*, met goede Weiden, en een menigte van Koebeesten in de zelve; 't geen my zo vreemd, als aangenaam, voorkwam. De Rivier loopt zeer sterk afwaarts, en heeft aan d'een zyde altemaal zand, allengskens opgeworpen, van de zelve gedaante, als het duinzand omtrent *Schevelingen*.'

In 1701 Cornelis de Bruijn left the Netherlands for a second journey, heading east. After a visit to the court of Tsar Peter the Great in Moscow, this new journey brought him to Persia. He visited the capital of the Achaemenid empire, Persepolis, where he made drawings of the palace ruins and of some of the great kings' tombs near the city and in nearby Naqš-e Rustam. On the façades, which have been carved into the rock slopes, the

Fig. 3 Delta landscape by Cornelis de Bruijn (De Bruijn 1698, plate 68, Allard Pierson, University of Amsterdam, KF 61-1401).

Fig. 4 Overview of the tombs at Naqš-e Rustam (De Bruijn 1714, plate 166, Allard Pierson, University of Amsterdam, OF 63-1098).

Fig. 5 Gobryas shown on the tomb of Darius I at Persepolis (after Schmidt 1970, plate 23).

far-reaching power of the Achaemenid empire is visualised (fig. 4). Rows of representatives of annexed regions, flanked by court members, are offering the great king gifts as a sign of surrender. All are depicted with characteristic dresses, facial features and hairstyles. One of the courtiers (fig. 5) reminded us of another small terracotta head of a man in the Allard Pierson collections, with the same provenance as the terracotta discussed above.

Persian or Greek?

The head (h. 6.7 cm, w. 5.2 cm) is hollow and moulded of beige clay (APM07192, fig. 6).[5] This portrait shows a man with tight curls rendered as carved stylised squares, and a short curly beard indicated by tiny round impressions. There are ample traces of black on the hair and beard. He is wearing a fillet to which an ornament – now missing, possibly a lotus flower – was attached above his forehead. He has almond-shaped, pronounced eyes and parts of the face are sloppily moulded, almost as if the object is not yet finished. The neck is heavy and bears traces of a painted necklace. The head can be dated to the Late Period (*c.* sixth-fifth century BC).

The first description of the object, written on the original Lunsingh Scheurleer inventory card, states 'The head of an "Asian"'. This is probably the interpretation by Von Bissing, from whom he bought the terracotta. Later on 'Asian' was corrected to 'Persian(?)', possibly by Lunsingh Scheurleer. To complicate the matter, in the guide to the Allard Pierson collection written by Lunsingh Scheurleer in 1937, the head is

5 Coll. Von Bissing T 271. Lunsingh Scheurleer 1937, 43, no. 353; Henkelman 2010, 7 fig. 3.

Fig. 6 Portrait of a Persian courtier. Terracotta, Memphis (Egypt), 5th-4th century BC, image Allard Pierson, University of Amsterdam, APM07192.

described as ‘maybe a Greek’.[6] The Allard Pierson Museum inventory book and card, written after the objects came to Amsterdam in 1934, also state ‘Greek(?)’ without further explanation.

Working on this article, we took a closer look at this remarkable portrait. Comparing the coiffure and fillet on this head with those of the peoples depicted on the Persian monuments indicates that this kind of curly hair is characteristic of Persian representatives. The fillet is also found in the representations of Persian courtiers, for example Gobryas (possibly the son of Mardonius, a general in the Persian wars with the Greeks), who is standing behind the Great King Darius I (522-485 BC) (fig. 5). The central ornament of the fillet which might have been a flower, is found on some other terracotta heads as well. These are interpreted as great kings, because of their longer beards. The terracotta head in the Allard Pierson, however, has a short beard similar to the depiction of Gobryas. Therefore we propose to interpret this portrait as a Persian courtier.

Currently there is much academic discussion on the influence of the Persian presence in Egypt and there is still much research to be done. The ongoing discussions on diversity in Antiquity and the relationship between the cultures of ancient Egypt, the Near East and the Greek world are very much alive as well. These two heads in the Allard Pierson show that Persians were portrayed by local Egyptian craftsmen. The naturalistic style may have been inspired by the Persians, who were proud of the diverse populations in their empire

6 Lunsingh Scheurleer 1937, 43, no. 353.

and who made efforts to distinguish them, and by the Greeks who were present in the Delta at the time.

To conclude: the discussed objects not only represent the diversity of cultures in the Delta of the sixth and fifth centuries BC, but also Willem's and our departments – Egypt, the ancient Near East and the Greek world. This short paper underlines the necessity for continuous investigation and reinterpretation of our collections. The new academic discourse provides us with the tools to look afresh at well-known objects. Unfortunately, Willem will soon retire from his curatorial duties; luckily the collections will leave us with many opportunities for new discoveries and research.

Bibliography

Bissing, F.W. von, 1930, Totenstele eines persischen Großen aus Memphis, *Zeitschrift der Morgenländische Gesellschaft* 84, 226-238.

Bruyn, C. de, 1698, *Reizen van Cornelis* de Bruyn, Door de vermaardste Deelen van *Klein Asia, De Eylanden Scio, Rhodus, Cyprus, Metelino, Stanchio &c. Mitsgaders de voornaamste Steden van Ægypten, Syrien en Palestina, Verrijkt met meer als 200. kopere Konstplaaten, vertoonende de beroemdste Landschappen, Steden, &c. Alles door den Autheur selfs na het leven afgetekend,* Delft.

Bruyn, C. de, 1702, *A voyage to the Levant: or Travels* in the principal parts of Asia Minor, the Islands of Scio, Rhodes, Cyprus, &c. : With an account of the most considerable cities of Egypt, Syria and the Holy Land. *Enrich'd with above two hundred copper-plates ... all drawn to the life,* London.

Bruin, C. de, 1714, *Reizen over Moskovie, door Persie en Indie: Verrykt met Driehondert kunstplaten, Vertoonende De beroemste lantschappen en steden, ook de byzondere dragten, beesten, gewassen en planten, die daar gevonden worden: Voor al derzelver oudheden, En welvoornamentlyk heel uitvoerig, die van het Heerlyke en van oudts de geheele werrelt door befaemde Hof van Persepolis, By den Persianen Tchilminar genaemt,* Amsterdam.

Colburn, H., 2020, *Archaeology of Empire in Achaemenid Egypt,* Edinburgh.

Haarlem, W.M. van, Lunsingh Scheurleer, R.A., 1986, *Gids voor de afdeling Egypte,* Amsterdam.

Henkelman, W.F.M., 2010, Alexander en de Perzen, *Allard Pierson Mededelingen* 103, 6-9.

Lunsingh Scheurleer, C.W., 1937, *Algemeene gids, Allard Pierson Museum, archaeologisch museum der Universiteit van Amsterdam Sarphatistraat 129-131,* Amsterdam.

Lunsingh Scheurleer, R.A., 1974, Quelques terres cuites Memphites, *Revue d'Égyptologie* 26, 83-99.

Lunsingh Scheurleer, R.A, 1992, *Egypte, geschenk van de Nijl,* Steenwijk.

Petrie, W.M.F., 1909, *Memphis I,* London.

Rehm, E., 2006, „Auf zu den Ufern des Nils" Vorderasiatica in Ägypten im 1. Jahrtausend v. Chr., *Ugarit-Forschungen* 37, 491-516.

Schmidt, E.F., Hauser, E.R. (ed.), 1970, *Persepolis III. The royal tombs and other monuments,* Chicago.

About the authors

Geralda Jurriaans-Helle (1955) studied Classics and Mediterranean Archaeology at the University of Amsterdam. She has been curator of the departments Greek world and Ancient Near East at the Allard Pierson since 1988 and will retire in 2021. She obtained her PhD in 2017 with the thesis *Composition in Athenian Black-figure Vase-painting: The 'Chariot in Profile'* Type Scene.

Laurien de Gelder (1988) studied Mediterranean Archaeology at the University of Amsterdam and has been part of the curatorial team Archaeological Collections at the Allard Pierson since 2016. She curated several of the renewed (2020) galleries and will succeed Geralda as curator of the Greek world and the Ancient Near East in 2021.

Once again about the term *nw*[1]

Galina A. Belova

In the ancient Egyptian capital Memphis on the edge of the Nile Delta William Matthew Flinders Petrie excavated the palace of Apries. Petrie uncovered a limestone block with inscriptions on both sides. This block was published in 1909[2] and is now kept in the Fitzwilliam Museum in Cambridge (fig. 1).[3] In this contribution the function of the monument of which this block was originally a part will be investigated.

Two officials

Bernard Bothmer first compared the block that is now in Cambridge to another one kept in the Brooklyn Museum in 1960 (fig. 2).[4] He emphasised that they correspond closely and that the representations differ only minutely. The names of two kings are mentioned in the inscriptions on the blocks: Amasis and Nectanebo I. The latter is described as alive and well, which provides a clear dating of the reliefs.

After Bothmer's publication both blocks were considered to be parts of a single structure. The inscriptions were first translated and commented on by Karl Jansen-Winkeln in 1997.[5] The content of the inscriptions is very difficult to understand because the grammatical rules of the Late Period are highly complex. The fact that some phrases seem meaningless points to the semi-cryptographic style that is characteristic of the early 30th dynasty.[6] The man who left the inscriptions, however, was a 'personal royal scribe' and must have had access to the best examples of grammar rules that existed at that time.

---

1 I would like to express my gratitude to Yekaterina Barbash, the curator of ECANEA of the Brooklyn Museum, for her help in preparing my article.

2 Petrie 1909, 13 pl. XVII, XXV (on the right).

3 Petrie 1909, 13. The block is kept in the Fitzwilliam Museum (Cambridge E.5.1909) as a donation from the British School of Archaeology in Egypt.

4 The Brooklyn Museum, Brooklyn, N.Y.; 56.152. Bothmer 1960, 92-94 Nr. 74, pl. 70-71, fig. 181-184.

5 Jansen-Winkeln 1997, 169-178 figs. 1, 2, 3 and 4 pl. XX, XXI and XXII. Jansen-Winkeln corrected some errors in the original drawing. J. Quaegebeur translated two short paragraphs from both texts in his monograph (Quaegebeur 1975, 156). The translation of the inscriptions from German to English was made by M. Cannata (Cannata 2020, 439).

6 Klotz 2010, 138.

in: Bercken, B.J.L. van den, 2021. *Egyptian Delta archaeology. Short studies in honour of Willem van Haarlem*, Leiden: Sidestone Press, pp. 95-101.

Fig. 1 Limestone block found by Petrie (height 126 cm, width 34 cm, thickness 14 cm), Cambridge E.5.1909. Image The Fitzwilliam Museum, CC-BY-NC-ND.

Fig. 2 Limestone block in the Brooklyn Museum (height 126.8 cm, width 34.7 cm, thickness 17.8 cm) Brooklyn, N.Y.; 56.152. Image Brooklyn Museum, CC-BY.

The inscriptions are a fictional dialogue between the author of the inscriptions, the 'personal royal scribe' Tjai-iset-n-imu (*ṯ3i-3ś.t-n-i͗m.w*), a contemporary of Nectanebo I, and the 'chief of the hall' Iahmes-sa-Neith (*i͗ʿḥ-mś-s3-nt*) who lived one-and-a-half centuries earlier, during the reign of Amasis. In exchange for renovating a building of Iahmes-sa-Neith and erecting a chapel for their 'united spirits' Tjai-iset-n-imu asks Iahmes-sa-Neith to ensure that the gods grant Nectanebo I a long reign. Iahmes-sa-Neith listens and reassures Tjai-iset-n-imu that the great god (Osiris) approves of his good deeds and will contribute to a long life for Nectanebo I.

Function and location of the structure

The key question is: what kind of 'construction' is meant in the texts? According to Petrie the Cambridge block was brought from a tomb.[7] Bothmer believed that the block was moved from a chapel, but he could not specify the nature of this construction.[8] Jansen-Winkeln agreed with Petrie that the Cambridge (and the Brooklyn) block come from a tomb of the Saite Period reused in the 30th dynasty.[9] He concludes that the inscriptions themselves confirm that the construction mentioned was a tomb, based on the following arguments: 1. the phrase *iri͗.n.nw* refers to the construction of the tomb, because it had this meaning in the Old Kingdom; 2. the *i͗m3ḫ* status is related to the care and provision of the tomb, because this term is often found with this meaning; 3. the fact that Iahmes-sa-Neith in order to comply with the request of Tjai-iset-n-imu goes to the necropolis and reports to Osiris explicitly indicates that the 'construction' is related to a tomb; and 4. the desire of Tjai-iset-n-imu to become one with Iahmes-sa-Neith after old age as well as the mention of the unity of their spirits suggest that the officials were buried in the same tomb.

The find location of the Cambridge block might favour a different interpretation of both inscriptions. Jansen-Winkeln used only a part of Petrie's description of the find location: 'in the south-west corner of the palace'.[10] Petrie described the location more precisely as 'in the south-west corner of the palace, under the tower.'[11] The key phrase is 'under the tower', which pinpoints the block's findspot under one of the structures of the Apries palace. According to Petrie the nature of the structures in the south-west corner of the palace is not clear. Nevertheless, the three narrow passages with very thick walls led him to conclude that the tower stood there.[12]

Unfortunately, Petrie did not record a more detailed description of the site of discovery of the block, he only pointed out that the block was used 'in reconstruction along with brickwork.' The moulding on the reverse side of the block was broken away to make the block fit in a new structure. It is known that the interior rooms of the palace of the Saite kings were decorated with limestone blocks.[13] So it is not surprising that the Cambridge block has been used as stone lining. That is what is important: this block was not a separate

---

7 Petrie 1909, 13.

8 Bothmer 1960, 92.

9 Jansen-Winkeln 1997, 169 and 175-176.

10 Jansen-Winkeln 1997, 169. The palace of Apries is situated in the north-eastern part of Memphis. In 2007 the Russian Academy was granted permission to excavate the palace of Apries.

11 Petrie 1909, 13.

12 Petrie 1909, 4.

13 Petrie 1909, pl. XIII.

artefact but rather a part of the palace decoration. The Brooklyn and Cambridge blocks could have been used to decorate the rooms of the palace of Apries.[14]

Discussion

There are no descriptions in the texts that would accurately determine the nature of the structures built by Iahmes-sa-Neith and Tjai-iset-n-imu. It is impossible to relate 'it' to the tomb (*nw*) with confidence. The expression *iri nw* could apply not only to the construction of the tomb but also to other structures,[15] including dedicatory ones.[16] Tjai-iset-n-imu explicitly states that he made the renovations where Iahmes-sa-Neith worked as 'the overseer of the portal': 'at your place in the great hall', which is in the palace. Another structure made by Tjai-iset-n-imu is named *ꜥḥ.t*.[17] The exact nature of this structure is unclear, but the term has to do with the king's administration. It was probably the king's office.[18]

Tjai-iset-n-imu's request to prolong the life of King Nectanebo concerned the living King, whose official residence was in all probability situated in the former palace of the Saite kings. It is well known that the rulers of the 30th dynasty emulated the glory of Saite times and restored Saite constructions. The royal administration of the Late Period, including the king's office, was housed in the palace of the Saite kings, which is confirmed by the find location of the Cambridge block and the results of excavations carried out by the Russian team in the territory of the palace of Apries and the so-called military camp.[19]

The word *imꜣḫ.w* is used in both texts with the meaning of 'merits'. These merits are also referred to as *biꜣ.w*, meaning 'good deeds'.[20] Tjai-iset-n-imu regards both terms as the 'legacy' of Iahmes-sa-Neith on earth. This legacy could not be anything other than his 'good deeds': merits that glorified the official and were remembered by his descendants.

The phrase '(I) went commending your name in the necropolis' should be understood as it is. Iahmes-sa-Neith 'went' to the necropolis. It means that he was not in the necropolis, occupying one of the tombs, but that his spirit 'lived' in the palace together with Tjai-iset-n-imu. From the context of the inscription however it follows that the connection with the necropolis must be close. Indeed, Petrie emphasised that the mound with the ruins of the palace gives a good view for observation up and down the Nile flood plain.[21] This means that for the inhabitants of the palace the entire necropolis was visible. Even today the Saqqara necropolis is perfectly visible from the palace. This sacred landscape allows the spirit to communicate directly with spirits of the dead and gods of the necropolis, and above all with Osiris who ruled there.

---

14 Bothmer indicated Mit Rahina as its provenience (Bothmer 1960, 93); both blocks are listed with other blocks which were found in Mit Rahina in Porter-Moss' Topographical Bibliography (PM III2, 831, 874); in the Brooklyn Museum's catalogue its provenience is uncertain (Fazzini et al. 1989, Nr. 78).

15 Wb II, 216, 6.

16 Wb II, 216, 9.

17 The term denotes the palace (Wb I, 214, 10,22), as well as 'the place where the administration is situated' (Wb I, 214, 11).

18 Probably the room is similar to what is represented on the wall of the tomb of 'scribe of memoranda of the good god' Tchaj (Borchardt 1907, 59 Abb. 1).

19 Belova (forthcoming a).

20 *bi3.w* 'amazing thing' (Wb I, 440); *bi*, *bit* 'good deeds' (Faulkner 1976, 80).

21 Petrie 1909, 4.

The important role played by 'guardian spirits' (*špst*) mentioned on both sides of the blocks cannot be overlooked. The names of spirits are mentioned on the outer side of Tjai-iset-n-imu's inscription: *ꜥnḫt* and *Smzt*. The text states that the spirits merged into one. The role played by spirits is described in the example of the spirit of Tjai-iset-n-imu. His spirit is represented on both reverse sides, bearing the same name as his wet-nurse *Smzt*, who cared for the house. Her personification not only breastfed Tjai-iset-n-imu but raised him as well, taking care of his health and sustenance. In our case the purpose of the spirits seems more defined, and two spirits become one but for all that the spirit of Iahmes-sa-Neith had to pass his heroism on to another official, perhaps through the milk of their wet-nurse. That is not about helping to overcome the horrors of the afterlife, but about the practical use of the glory of the heroic predecessor.

Conclusion

In the inscriptions Tjai-iset-n-imu reports that he has done Iahmes-sa-Neith a great favour by restoring his place in the great hall where the latter worked. In return Tjai-iset-n-imu asked for the protection of Iahmes-sa-Neith, who was known for his glorious deeds. For this purpose, Tjai-iset-n-imu built a special room in the palace, where, through the union of spirits, he associated himself with this great dignitary from the past and, like him, continued to do good deeds.

There is no doubt that the Cambridge and Brooklyn blocks originally framed a doorway, as they were decorated on both sides. Therefore, it can be assumed that the 'great hall' was connected to a room meant for guardian spirits. In these rooms the spirits of the two officials came together: working in the 'great hall' and spiritually united in the second room.

It is known that the Saite pharaohs ordered extensive renovations after expelling their enemies from the country.[22] The pharaohs of the 30th dynasty followed the policy of the Saite kings and rebuilt the Egyptian state after the destruction inflicted by the Persians. The devastation caused by the Persians not only affected temples and religious activities but also the administrative buildings. The palace of Apries where the Persian administration was housed was damaged as well.[23] Nectanebo I and Nectanebo II 'purified' monuments. It was a period of intensive reconstruction throughout Egypt, accompanied by rich benefactions. The inscriptions on the blocks indicate that the reconstruction of the palace could have taken place during the reign of Nectanebo I or later.

Thus, the proposed interpretation gives rise to a new reading of religious and mystical representations of the Egyptians. It is not only about overcoming the barriers of the underworld, but also about the practical use of spirits. For example, some spirits help to get a promotion and others guard a person's health to achieve this goal. The texts tell us about the Egyptian belief in affiliating oneself with the spirit of an important person for protection, but also about using them for personal purposes. Only new evidence can confirm the validity of these observations.

22 Klotz 2010, 128.

23 Belova (forthcoming b).

Bibliography

Borchardt, L., 1907, Das Dienstgebäude des Auswärtigen Amtes unter den Ramessiden, *Zeitschrift für Ägyptische Sprache und Altertumskunde* 44, 59-61.

Bothmer, B.W., 1960, *Egyptian Sculpture of the Late Period, 700 B.C. to A.D. 100*, New York.

Belova, G.A., (fortcoming a), "White walls" is the core of Memphis.

Belova G.A., (forthcoming b), Herodotus' "White fortress".

Cannata, M., 2020, *Three hundred years of death: the Egyptian funerary industry in the Ptolemaic period. Culture and history of the ancient Near East,* Boston.

Faulkner, R.O., 1976, *A Concise Dictionary of Middle Egyptian*, Oxford.

Fazzini, R.A., Bianchi, R.S., Romano, J.F., Spanel, D.B., 1989, *Ancient Egyptian Art in the Brooklyn Museum*, New York.

Jansen-Winkeln, K., 1996, Zu den Denkmälern des Erziehers Psametiks II, *Mitteilungen des Deutschen Archäologischen Instituts, Abteilung Kairo* 52, 187-199.

Jansen-Winkeln, K., 1997, Eine Grabübernahme in der 30. Dynastie, *Journal of Egyptian Archaeology* 83, 169-178.

Klotz, D., 2010, Two Studies on the Late Period Temples at Abydos, *Bulletin de l'Institut français d'archéologie orientale* 110, 127-163.

Meulenaere, H. De, 1985, Un notable Mendésien de la 26e Dynastie, in Posener- Kriéger, P. (ed.) *Mélanges Gamal Eddin Mokhtar, I. Bibliothèque d'Étude* 97, 187-197.

Petrie, W.M.F., 1909, *The Palace of Apries (Memphis II)*, London.

Porter, B., Moss, R.L., 1978, *Topographical Bibliography of Ancient Egyptian Hieroglyphic texts, reliefs, and paintings, III.2, Memphis*, Oxford.

Quaegebeur, J., 1975, *Le dieu égyptien Shaï. Orientalia Lovaniensia Analecta* 2, Leuven.

Quirke, St., 2004, *Titles and bureaux of Egypt 1850-1700 BC*, London.

Ranke, H., 1935, *Die Ägyptischen Personennamen*, Bd.1, Glückstadt.

Scharff, A., 1938, Ein Spätzeitrelief des Berliner Museum, *Zeitschrift für Ägyptische Sprache und Altertumskunde* 74, 41-49.

Sethe, K., 1907, *Urkunden der 18. Dynastie*, Leipzig.

Staehelin, E., 1986, Tracht, *Lexikon der Ägyptologie VI*, 726-737.

Velde, H. te, 1982, Mittler, *Lexikon der Ägyptologie IV*, 161-163.

Vercoutter, J., 1949, Les statues du général Hor, gouverneur d'Hérakléopolis, de Busiris et d'Héliopolis (Louvre A.88, Alexandrie, s.n.) [avec 5 planches]. *Bulletin de l'Institut français d'archéologie orientale* 49, 85-114.

Ward, W., 1982, Old Kingdom sS a n nsw n xft-Hr, "Personal Scribe of Royal Records" and Middle Kingdom sS a n nsw n xft-Hr, "Scribe of Royal Tablet of the Court, *Orientalia* 51, 382-389.

About the author

Galina A. Belova's doctoral thesis is titled *Ancient Egypt and Neighboring Countries* (1995). Belova was the director of the Centre for Egyptological Studies of the Russian Academy of Sciences (2000-2017) and now is the Centre's research director. She took part in joint Russian-Dutch expeditions at Tell Ibrahim Awad and was co-director of the Russian-German expedition to TT320 in Luxor. Belova is the head of the Russian archaeological mission in Memphis and the editor-in-chief of the journal *Egypt and the Surrounding World* (in Russian). She is a member of many international scholarly societies.

A glass *ba* bird in the Allard Pierson

René van Beek

Introduction

The archaeological collection of the Allard Pierson is very diverse and over the past decades curators have been researching a wide variety of objects. Sometimes objects acquire a new meaning through research, sometimes even the description of the object has to be changed. A critical look can provide new insights. Recently a new surprise came to light, because for this contribution I went looking for an object in which Willem's and my fields of interest touch.[1]

Ba with different layers

My eye was caught by an Egyptian glass *ba* bird, an extraordinary object that has been in the museum collection since 1934 (fig. 1). The object is almost 8 cm high and has the appearance of a bird with a human head covered by a wig. It is made of solid red glass and partly covered with a yellowish weathering layer.

The information on the inventory card tells us that Lunsingh Scheurleer acquired this object in 1921 from Friedrich Wilhelm Freiherr von Bissing's collection. It was described as stone and had inventory number S112. Scheurleer also considered it to be made of stone and described it as 'bird of the soul', but it also reminded him of a Siren. When the bird came into the Scheurleer collection it was covered with a paraffin and lacquer layer, according to his inventory card. This must have made the glass surface invisible and may have been the reason why Von Bissing and Lunsingh Scheurleer thought it was stone.

Apparently, doubt had arisen in the museum history of the object, because the inventory card of the Allard Pierson mentions as material: 'brown green glass?' A restoration report from 1969 shows that from the surface layer, consisting of a yellowish weathering layer supplemented with lacquer and paraffin, the paraffin was removed and replaced by a thin layer of plaster. This plaster was then repainted to give the entire surface a brownish yellow colour. In 2020 the plaster layer was removed and the red glass became visible. The surface of the bird is still partially covered with the yellowish weathering layer, which of course will not be removed.

1 I would like to thank Ben van den Bercken for his valuable advice on the *ba*.

in: Bercken, B.J.L. van den, 2021. *Egyptian Delta archaeology. Short studies in honour of Willem van Haarlem*, Leiden: Sidestone Press, pp. 103-106.

Egyptian glass

When talking about Egyptian glass, one often thinks of small glassware made of core glass as it occurs from the 18th dynasty. The earliest Egyptian glass may have originated as an unintentional product in the production of faience, and perhaps that earliest glass was created by faience makers.[2] It is often assumed that glass was made in Egypt itself as early as the Amarna period from raw materials such as sand, lime and soda. But it is certainly also possible that the Egyptians imported and melted glass ingots to make products. This would mean a secondary use of glass. Von Bissing notes that Egypt was an important centre for glassware and figurines in the pharaonic period, unlike regions such as Syria and Lebanon, where glass was invented but where large-scale production of small containers only started in Roman times.[3] The Egyptians used glass not only for small containers but also for small sculptures, beads and amulets. The making of glass figurines or small sculptures is considered an Egyptian invention. The earliest examples go back to the time of Amenhotep II in the fifteenth century BC, while glass production on a broader scale already started under Thutmosis III.

In the 18th dynasty there are glass sculptures of high quality. Few examples have been preserved from that early period, however, and probably glass was replaced by faience or glassy faience, substances that are suitable for making sculptures mainly because of their great flexibility. In the Late Period and the Ptolemaic period in particular, this high quality of glass figurines decreases and subsequently we see mainly glass inlays and few freestanding figures.

It seems likely that our *ba* bird was made according to the so-called lost-wax method. That means that the figure is initially made from wax and then covered with a very fine clay. After firing the clay – with the wax running out of the mould – the mould was filled with cast glass. After the glass had solidified, the fired clay was broken away and the glass sculpture emerged. Details on the surface might have been applied after the casting process. Because of the weathering layer that is present on the Amsterdam *ba* bird, no seams of the mould can be discerned. The colour of the glass was obtained by the addition of metal compounds. Red glass is notoriously difficult to make and copper compounds probably play a role in obtaining the colour.

Two birds

Freestanding glass sculptures in the form of a *ba* bird are rare. In earlier periods they are mainly found as amulets and in the Ptolemaic period also as flat inlays.[4] *Ba* birds of about the same size and posture as the Amsterdam *ba* are also found in bronze.[5] These freestanding *ba* birds seem, because of their size, not to have been meant as portable amulets but served as less movable objects, possibly on a tomb stela or mummy coffin. In the Amsterdam specimen a small bulge is visible at the bottom. It appears to be a means to attach the bird to

---

2 Nicholson/Shaw 2000, 195.

3 Von Bissing 1908, 211.

4 For the *ba* as an amulet: e.g. National Museum of Antiquities, Leiden inventory number F 2015/9.121. As a Ptolemaic period inlay e.g. the Metropolitan Museum, New York accession number 17.194.2486. See Casini 2015, 10 for an excellent overview of parallels in different materials.

5 For a metal *ba* bird, e.g. the Israel Museum, Jerusalem accession number 97.063.0110. See also Casini 2015, 10 for an excellent overview of parallels in different materials.

Fig. 1 Ba bird. Glass, h. 7.7 cm, w. 3.2 cm. Ptolemaic period, c.250-50 BC, image Allard Pierson, University of Amsterdam, APM07968.

something. It is impossible to say whether this was on a stela or on a mummy coffin in order to allow the *ba* ('spirit') of the deceased to re-enter the world of the living.

In the collection of the British Museum is a close parallel for the Amsterdam *ba* bird.[6] The London bird is also made of opaque red glass, is a few millimetres bigger and has the same posture, in which details such as the feathers are clearly visible. This British Museum *ba* comes from Achmim in central Egypt and is dated to the Ptolemaic period. It is plausible that the Amsterdam bird, whose archaeological origins unfortunately are unknown, comes from that same period.

Siren, *ba* and Willem

A *ba* bird is represented as a bird with a human head and sometimes arms. The Amsterdam bird's only human characteristic is its head. The appearance of our bird made Lunsingh Scheurleer think of a Siren. There are obvious physical similarities between a Siren and a *ba*, but they are also both associated with death: in ancient Egypt the *ba* as a representation of the deceased re-entering the world of the living via the tomb, and in ancient Greece, whoever heard a Siren had to die... With their sweet and seductive voices, Sirens are therefore completely different in character from *ba* birds.

Ba birds are common in museum collections, but glass specimens are rare. Curators of Egyptian collections are also fairly common, but Willem van Haarlem is unique. I would like to thank him for managing the Egyptian collection as he has done for decades. We are going to miss Willem, but just like a *ba* bird that can move freely, he will probably come back once in a while! Just as the *ba* continues life after death, the spirit of Willem will still be present after his farewell to the museum!

---

6 British Museum, London, museum number EA64341.

Bibliography

Bissing, F. W. de, 1908, Sur l'histoire du verre en Égypte, *Revue archéologique, quatrième série* 11, 211-221.

Casini, E., 2015, The three-dimensional representations of the human-headed ba-bird: some remarks about their origin and function, *Egitto e Vicino Oriente*, Vol. 38 , 9-32.

Cooney, J.D., 1976, *Catalogue of Egyptian Antiquities in the British Museum (Vol. IV – Glass)*, London.

Nicholson, P.T., Shaw, I., 2000, *Ancient Egyptian materials and Technology*, Cambridge.

Riefstahl, E., 1968, *Ancient Egyptian glass and glazes in the Brooklyn Museum*, Brooklyn.

Taylor, J., 2001, *Death and the afterlife in Ancient Egypt*, London.

About the author

René van Beek is curator of the Classical department and the collection of plaster casts of the Allard Pierson. He is currently working on a catalogue of the Roman glass collection.

Neilos and Euthenia

Robert Lunsingh Scheurleer

Introduction

The majestic sight of Egypt's fountain of life leaves few modern visitors unimpressed. People from Antiquity were equally awestruck at the sight of the Nile. The yearly inundation brought fertility to a land that stretched over more than a thousand kilometres and culminated in the Delta. In that region Willem van Haarlem investigated aspects of Egypt's ancient roots. In this contribution attention is given to some representations of the river and of its female counterpart Euthenia some three millennia later. The Egyptians saw the river and the life it contained as divine, venerating it as the god Hapy whose female breasts refer to his nourishing power.

Fig. 1 Statue of Neilos, limestone, image Allard Pierson, University of Amsterdam, APM07827.

in: Bercken, B.J.L. van den, 2021. *Egyptian Delta archaeology. Short studies in honour of Willem van Haarlem*, Leiden: Sidestone Press, pp. 107-112.

Neilos

To the newcomers in the Graeco-Roman period, the appearance of Hapy must have been one more among so many other enigmatic aspects of the country. The importance of the river, however, most certainly escaped nobody. Consequently 'Neilos', the god of the river shaped according to Greek idiom, was introduced. Since the Renaissance he is best known from the colossal Roman sculptural version: a reclining statue with a *himation* (mantle) around his legs and leaning on an Egyptian sphinx. He is surrounded by lively *putti* (cupids) that stand for the number of cubits the river may rise.[1] Danielle Bonneau collected an impressive amount of epigraphical and archaeological documentation on the subject.[2] For centuries this Alexandrian rendering of the Nile inspired representations of river gods.[3] The Roman Nile however has Hellenistic antecedents.

In Hellenistic Egypt the god of the river was shown leaning on a characteristic river occupant: the hippopotamus. An example in Stuttgart represents this earlier version.[4] A limestone version of a similar Neilos including the hippopotamus was acquired by Friedrich Wilhelm Freiherr von Bissing (1873-1956) in Alexandria (fig. 1).[5] As with pharaonic Hapy, aquatic plants and animals point to the creative force of the water. The buds of the white lotus crowning the head of Graeco-Roman Neilos have a similar function. As to the god's hanging breast, is this a legacy of the pharaonic image of the god Hapy? In the ancient Near East and Egypt such corpulency was (and still is) a sign of prosperity and opulence.

Neilos holding a *cornucopia* (horn of plenty) and reclining on a crocodile figures in some varieties on imperial Alexandrian coins of Hadrian (fig. 2).[6] Other coins of the same emperor show only the bust of the god with a *cornucopia*, as *pars pro toto* for his integral image. He is identified by the two lotus buds on his head (fig. 3).[7]

Fig. 2 Neilos on a crocodile, reverse of Alexandrian drachm of Hadrian, private collection (image Josephine van den Berg).

Fig. 3 Bust of Neilos, reverse of Alexandrian tetradrachm of Hadrian, private collection (image Josephine van den Berg).

1 This statue is in the Vatican, see Helbig 1963, no. 440 (W. Fuchs).
2 Bonneau 1964; Parlasca 1966, 155-157.
3 Haskell/Penny 1982, no. 65 and fig. 142.
4 Fuchs 1969, 316-317, fig. 352.
5 Moormann 2000, no. 30, pl. 13c-d.
6 Hadrian, bronze drachm, the year not visible anymore.
7 Billon tetradrachm, year 19 (AD 134-135), Milne 1971, no. 1454.

Emblemata of Neilos

The most characteristic features of Neilos can also be found on a number of small faience busts of the god. On a faience example from a private collection two lotus buds crowning a small bearded man wearing a mantle over his right shoulder identify bountiful Neilos (fig. 4). The shiny surface of this bust has been fired a greenish blue. A second bust of the same type is in the Allard Pierson collection and was formerly with Von Bissing (fig. 5).[8] The colour of this bust has faded to yellowish. Both busts stem from closely related moulds. A third bust is in the Akademisches Kunstmuseum, Bonn. It was tentatively identified as Isis.[9] Finally, when shown the Neilos of fig. 4, Lucas Benaki remarked that a similar example could be found in his collection.

These busts were clearly made in series and even more may have survived. On the convex back below the shoulders the bust does not have a glassy surface. It seems to have broken off from a support that was probably located on the inside of a cup.[10] The head must have been free from the background. Such *emblemata* stand in a long tradition of translating versions of precious metal (for example silver) to affordable materials. They must have served in the cults of gods, in this case Neilos.[11]

Fig. 4 Bust of Neilos, faience, height 5.42 cm, nose damaged, private collection (image Josephine van den Berg).

Fig. 5 Bust of Neilos, faience, height 5.14 cm, image Allard Pierson, University of Amsterdam, APM07570.

8 Von Bissing inventory number F. 212.
9 Schmidt 1997, no. 214, Inv. D 735, pl. 67.
10 Compare Nenna 2005, no. 502.
11 Bonneau 1964, 398-401.

The primordial importance of the level of the flood of the Nile was known all over the ancient world.[12] Offerings to the river, edible and sometimes precious, are well documented.[13] The river encouraged the birth of boys who would consequently be called Neilodoros and the like, if not simply River.[14] A Nile festival, and certainly not the last one, is recorded as late as AD 424.[15] A certain Theodoulos, who ordered a supply of wine for that occasion, suggests that the river was celebrated both by people of the old and of the new (Christian) faith. The belief that the river required offerings to bring about its beneficent flood lived on and is of all times.[16]

The when and where of the manufacture of the Neilos busts is not clearly determined. The technique and colour of the bust in fig. 4 are identical to those of a well-preserved example of a Roman-Egyptian cylindrical vase, attributed to the first or second century.[17]

Euthenia

The female counterpart of Neilos (sometimes described as his daughter) is Euthenia, the personification of a successful harvest and of *abundantia*. As the 'granary of the empire' Egypt was closely controlled by the Roman emperors, who hoped for a successful harvest. A delicate relief of Neilos and Euthenia on the reflector of several terracotta oil lamps reminds us of representations of Danae and suggests a Hellenistic origin.[18]

A bronze drachm of the Alexandrian mint shows the shipping of corn under Antoninus Pius in his regnal year 18 (AD 154-155). On this coin Euthenia, with corn ears, is shown together with Tyche/Fortuna, who is holding a rudder. On either side of the goddesses is a ship: the one on the left arriving, that on the right sailing out.[19]

In Late Antiquity the iconography of the abundance of the Nile seems to loosen. Two figures on an ivory *pyxis* might represent Euthenia with the sphinx and Neilos amidst *putti*. The two are separated by a river with a lotus plant and a crocodile.[20]

Representations of Euthenia on coins are limited to a few emperors. Like Neilos, the goddess is usually shown reclining on a sphinx. A rare bronze drachm struck under Antoninus Pius, year 3 (AD 139-140) mentions her name.[21]

Discussing a marble statue of 'Demeter/Isis' or 'the Egyptian Demeter' in Boston, John J. Herrmann reminds us of the grouping of Demeter facing Euthenia on Alexandrian coins.[22] Joseph G. Milne described a coin in Oxford with a similar scene.[23] A coin similar to a coin in Boston and formerly in the Art Institute in Chicago can be seen in fig. 6.[24] The

---

12 From the time of Anastasius (AD 491-518) comes a silver *patera* with *putti* marking a Nilometer with the height of the flood (Collection Ermitage, Saint Petersburg).

13 Bowman 1986, 183.

14 Perdrizet 1921, 62.

15 Bagnall 1993, 270; P.Oxy. XLIII 3148.

16 El-Mouelhy 1956, 10-13.

17 On those vases: Grimm 1972, 71-100; e.g. Nenna 2005, 186 no. 502.

18 E.g. Perdrizet 1921, 62-63, no. 161. Alexandrian Euthenia in marble: Savvopoulos/Bianchi 2012, 151 pl. 47B inv. 24124.

19 Förstner 1987, Köln, no. 1749 (var.); Gorny & Mosch, Auction no. 208, Munich, 2012, lot no. 1891.

20 Wiesbaden Slg. Nassauischer Altertümer, inv. 7865. E.g. Von Falck/Lichtwark 1996, 199 no. 199 '6th century'.

21 Illustrated: Auction Gorny & Mosch, Munich, cat. no. 265, 2019, lot no. 1180.

22 Herrmann 1999, 70 and 121 no. 101 fig. 12.

23 Milne 1971, 136, s.v. Demeter.

24 Hadrian, year 18, AD 133-134. Formerly in the Art Institute, inv. 1980.909, now in a private collection.

Fig. 6 Euthenia and Demeter, reverse of Alexandrian drachm of Hadrian, private collection (image Josephine van den Berg).

Boston and Chicago coins are almost identical. Despite some damage visible between the goddesses, it is clear their dies have been made by capable artisans, which is evidenced by the realistic drapery. The nature of Euthenia can barely be more clearly expressed than by the attributes she is shown with.

The repertoire of artists in the Roman world, including die engravers, stood in a long and persistent tradition. Moreover, in Alexandria the theme of the human body leaning on a pillar had Ptolemaic origins.[25] The good quality of the Hadrianic coins is in accordance with Milne's observation of the work issued by the Alexandrian mint.[26] That goes certainly for the tetradrachm with the elegant bust of the bearded Neilos (fig. 3).

For the faithful, however, not the aesthetic quality of the image counts, but its religious significance. The veneration of Neilos, the Nile and its miraculous yearly flood expresses the deeply felt links between the divine and the communities living their lives along the river during successive generations and civilisations.

Bibliography

Bagnall, R.S., 1996, *Egypt in Late Antiquity*, Princeton.

Bonneau, D., 1964, *La crue du Nil, divinité égyptienne (332 av.-641 ap. J.-C.)*, Paris.

Bowman, A.K., 1986, *Egypt after the Pharaohs, 332 BC-AD 642, from Alexander to the Arab Conquest*, London.

Falck, M. von, Lichtwark, F., 1996, *Ägypten, Schätze aus dem Wüstensand*, Wiesbaden.

Förstner, G., 1987, *Die Münzen der römischen Kaiser in Alexandrien, Historisches Museum, Kleine Schriften* 35, Frankfurt am Main.

Fuchs, W., 1969, *Die Skulptur der Griechen*, München.

Gorny & Mosch: *Auctions Gorny & Mosch, Giessener Münzhandlung GmbH*, München.

Grimm, G., 1972, Two Early Imperial Faience Vessels from Egypt, *Miscellanea Wilbouriana I*, Mainz, 72-100.

Haskell, F., Penny, N., 1982, *Taste and the Antique. The Lure of Classical Sculpture, 1500-1900*, New Haven and London.

Helbig, W., 1963, *Führer durch die offentlichen Sammlungen klassischer Altertümer in Rom*, Tübingen.

25 Compare Vollenweider 1978, no. 376 with references.

26 Milne 1971, xl, par. 155.

Herrmann, J.J., 1999, Demeter-Isis or an Egyptian Demeter? A Graeco-Roman Sculpture from an Egyptian Workshop in Boston, *Jahrbuch des Deutschen Archäologischen Instituts* 114, 65-123.

Milne, J.G., 1971, *Catalogue of Alexandrian Coins, Ashmolean Museum,* Oxford and London.

Moormann, E.M., 2000, Ancient Sculpture in the Allard Pierson Museum Amsterdam, *Collections of the Allard Pierson Museum* 1, Amsterdam.

El-Mouelhy, I., 1956, La fiancée du Nil, *Egypt Travel Magazine*, no. 26, September 1956, 10-13.

Nenna, M.-D., 2005, En Égypte sous la domination Romaine, in Caubet, A., Pierrat-Bonnefois, G. (eds.), 2005, *Faïences de l'Antiquité, de l'Égypte à l'Iran*, Paris, 186.

Parlasca, K., 1966, Review of : Bonneau, D., La crue du Nil. Divinité égyptienne à travers mille ans d'histoire (332 av.-641 ap. J.-C.) d'après les auteurs grecs et latins, et les documents des époques Ptolémaique, romaine et byzantine, *Bibliotheca Orientalis XXIII*, 155-157.

Perdrizet, P., 1921, *Les terres cuites grecques d'Égypte de la collection Fouquet*, Paris.

Falck, M. von, Lichtwark, F. (eds.), 1996, *Ägypten, Schätze aus dem Wüstensand. Kunst und Kultur der Christen am Nil*, Wiesbaden.

Savvopoulos, K., Bianchi, R.S., 2012, *Graeco-Roman Museum I*, Alexandria.

Schmidt, S., 1997, *Katalog der ptolemäischen und kaiserzeitlichen Objekte aus Ägypten im Akademischen Kunstmuseum Bonn*, Munich.

Vollenweider, M.-L., 1978, Boardman, J., *Ashmolean Museum Oxford, Catalogue of the Engraved Gems and Finger Rings, I, Greek and Etruscan*, Oxford.

About the author

Robert Alexander Lunsingh Scheurleer became fascinated with Egyptian faience and the interaction between cultures in Antiquity by the discovery of a faience image of Alexander the Great with an Amsterdam art dealer. In 1968 he was admitted to the École pratique des hautes études in Paris, with archaeology, numismatics and Egyptology as orientations. He completed his PhD on Mit Rahineh faience at the Sorbonne in 1973. In 1976 he was appointed curator at the Allard Pierson Museum and from 2002 to his retirement he was its director. In the period 1993-1997 he was visiting professor for Greek art and archaeology at the University of Ghent. Among the memorable events in his career at the Allard Pierson was the gift by Nina van Leer of her father's Egyptian collection and the new presentation of the Egyptian collection with a focus on the Graeco-Roman and Coptic periods in 1992.

A Ptolemaic king as Egyptian pharaoh

Branko F. van Oppen de Ruiter

Introduction

Willem van Haarlem's Egyptological interests and mine could scarcely be any further apart: his predynastic, mine Graeco-Roman. Fortunately, we have easily found enough mutual interests beyond Egyptology to engage in many friendly conversations over the years. Perhaps our most heated discussion concerned the subject of the present contribution. As it represents a Ptolemaic king, it would best fit in the new Hellenistic gallery of the Allard Pierson, I argued. The counter-argument was that as a near-complete statue of an Egyptian pharaoh, it belongs in the new Egyptian rooms, then still in the planning stage. I hope Willem will appreciate this re-evaluation of the statue. I am certain that he will be delighted with this beautiful *Festschrift* in his honour, and wish him many more years of happiness.

A sculptural portrait of a Ptolemaic king in the guise of an Egyptian pharaoh graces the Hellenistic gallery of the Allard Pierson in Amsterdam (fig. 1).[1] This gallery named *From Alexander to Cleopatra* was opened in early 2017 (fig. 2). The statue was part of the collection of eminent Egyptologist F. W. Freiherr von Bissing, but its findspot or provenience is unknown.[2] There should be little doubt that the object originates from Egypt, perhaps Alexandria or Memphis. With its conventional pose but Macedonian royal subject, its un-Egyptian material but well-proportioned physique, should this statue be understood as Greek or Egyptian? And can evidence support attribution to Ptolemy VIII Euergetes II (*c*.184/3-116 BC)? These are some of the questions I would like to consider in this short contribution.

1 APM07780; ex F.W. von Bissing coll., inv. no. S.728; Bissing 1914, nos. 103-104, n. 14; Van Haarlem 1986, 25-27; Lunsingh Scheurleer/Van Haarlem 1986, 58, fig. 38; Lunsingh Scheurleer 1992, 101, pl. 63a-b; Stanwick 2003, cat. no. C12.

2 It was acquired from F.W. von Bissing by Museum Scheurleer, The Hague, in 1921, from which the Allard Pierson Museum obtained it in 1934.

in: Bercken, B.J.L. van den, 2021. *Egyptian Delta archaeology. Short studies in honour of Willem van Haarlem*, Leiden: Sidestone Press, pp. 113-120.

Fig. 1 Statue of a Ptolemaic king as Egyptian pharaoh, marble, 73 x 21.5 x 18.5 cm; unknown findspot, Egypt, image Allard Pierson, University of Amsterdam, APM07780.

Fig. 2 The statue on display in the Hellenistic gallery of the Allard Pierson, Amsterdam, at the time of installation. Image by the author; used with permission.

A Ptolemy in pharaonic guise

The half-life-size statue has been published in the first of Willem van Haarlem's comprehensive Corpus Antiquitatum Aegyptiacarum volumes.[3] Still, allow me to briefly describe it a little further (fig. 1). The king is standing stiffly in a striding pose with his left leg forward and his arms held straight along his body. He wears a plain *nemes* (head cloth) that is decorated with the *uraeus* (royal cobra). Apart from the *shendyt* (kilt) tied around the waist with a belt, the king is nude. He holds short rods in both hands. These rods are apparently undamaged and therefore not part of larger objects, such as *ankh* signs. The nature of these rods remains obscure. The figure has an uninscribed back pillar with trapezoid finial.

The statue has been preserved nearly complete with only the lower part broken away diagonally: the right foot and ankle and the whole lower left leg are missing. The lower end of the kilt's middle fold is gone. The upper part of the right side of the face and the nose are chipped off; the stone is cracked across the upper right side of the head; the cobra's head is missing; there is slight damage to the arms and some other surface damage. Some of the right front of the head cloth as well as the lower left arm have been restored. In short, the statue portrays an Egyptian pharaoh, who on stylistic grounds and material can be dated to the Ptolemaic period.

---

3 Van Haarlem 1986, 25-27 (CAA).

Hellenistic style features

Von Bissing and Van Haarlem already noted that the sculptural style was influenced by Greek art. The use of creamy marble with orange-brown veins is decidedly un-Egyptian. According to Stanwick's interpretation, the material itself points to an artist's workshop in

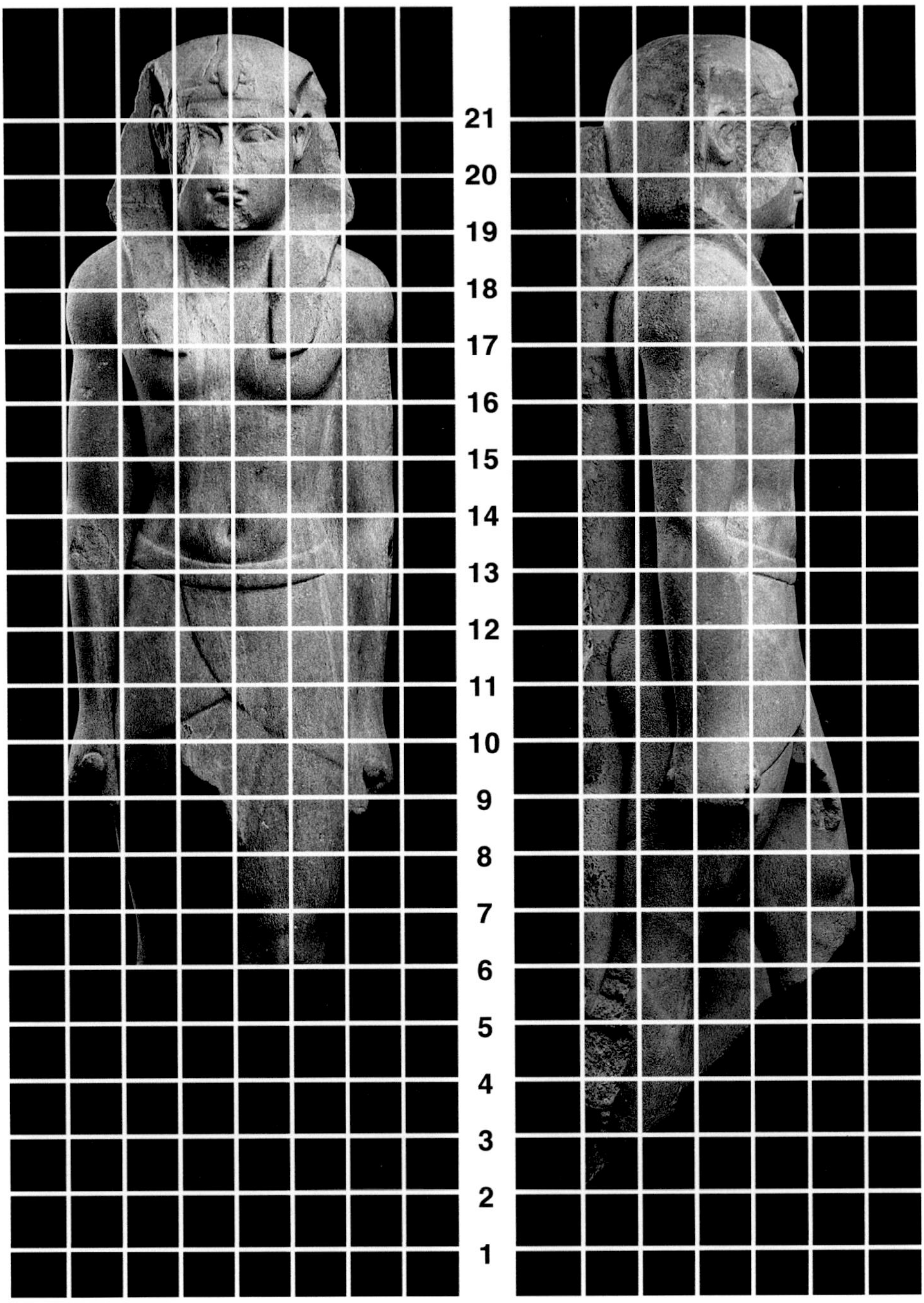

Fig. 3 APM07780 with overlaid proportional grid. Image by the author; photo Allard Pierson, University of Amsterdam.

a predominantly Greek city.[4] Style and material date the statue to the Hellenistic period, and identify the king as a member of the Ptolemaic dynasty. But does that mean that the sculptural style should be understood as Greek rather than Egyptian?

The stiff, striding pose with the arms beside the body is conventional in pharaonic Egyptian art. The stone between the arms and the body, and between the legs and the back pillar, has not been fully carved away to free the limbs, as one would expect in a Greek-style statue. The body is well proportioned, the musculature of the torso particularly athletic, but does it follow Greek or Egyptian ideals? Traditionally, pharaonic art since the 12th dynasty at the latest followed a canon of proportions for formal art.[5] This ideal was based on a grid of 18 squares from the sole of the foot to the hairline of a standing figure (god, king or official) and was applied in the formal art of temple and tomb reliefs. During the 25th dynasty, however, an innovative system based on 21 squares was introduced for standing figures from the sole of the foot to the upper eyelid.

How does the Ptolemaic pharaoh in Amsterdam fit in this proportional grid, in which the knee comes in the seventh square and the navel in the fourteenth? To answer this question, several difficulties should be taken into consideration. First, the statue is broken and the missing feet prevent a proper alignment of the baseline.[6] Second, the scholarly study of the Egyptian canon of proportions has understandably focused predominantly on temple and tomb reliefs of the Middle and New Kingdoms. The focus was rarely on statuary from the Late Period and Graeco-Roman period. Third, ancient Egyptian relief scenes do not normally show human figures in frontal view, but in an unnatural combination of frontal and profile views. Still, it has been established that grids were used throughout the Ptolemaic period, for example in the chapel of Ptolemy I at Tuna el-Gebel and the stela of Tentimhotep from Saqqara dating from the reign of Cleopatra VII.[7]

If we lay a grid on the Amsterdam statue, placing the top at the upper eyelids and what would be the seventh line from the base at the knee (fig. 3), the result shows that the statue adheres quite accurately to the expected proportional system. The navel is located just below line 14 at two-thirds of the statue, while the knees would have been at one-third of its height. The arms are each 10 squares in length of which the fist occupies one. The shoulders droop down from the nineteenth line. Four squares make up the face between the eyelids and the chin. All these dimensions are within the general Late Period canon of proportions.[8]

---

4 According to Stanwick (2003, 78-128), Alexandria and Canopus produced mainly high-quality colossal granite statuary in 'Greek' style; the Arsinoite nome produced medium-quality, life-size limestone statuary in 'provincial' style; while Upper Egypt produced medium- to high-quality, variously sized limestone or 'basalt' (dark stone) statuary in 'Egyptian' style. Stanwick does not explain how this geographic determination is made in the regular absence of provenience information, nor how he establishes his assessment of the quality and style of each statue.

5 Iversen 1975; Robins 1994.

6 Photographs of three-dimensional statues also create foreshortening effects due to perspective distortion.

7 Note that the squares of the grid applied in the chapel of Ptolemy in Tuna el-Gebel are not of exactly the same size. This indicates that while a grid system was in use, its absolute geometric accuracy was less relevant. This lack of accuracy complicates a scientific demonstration whether an Egyptian work of art adheres to the relevant canon of proportions or not. (An image is available online at http://hdl.library.upenn.edu/1017/d/fisher/n2003080048, accessed 23 Sept. 2020).

8 We can now calculate that the original height would have been approximately 80 cm.

We thus see a paradoxical combination of conservative, archaicising features with apparent innovative Egyptian as well as Greek inspiration. Observing that the statue is either Greek or Egyptian in style is therefore incorrect. It is neither Greek nor Egyptian. Designating the artwork's style as Graeco-Egyptian is not correct either, as it is not an obvious fusion of two art styles. The entanglements of conservative and innovative elements, of Greek and Egyptian aspects, of materials and artistic ideals of two cultural traditions would be better described as Hellenistic Egyptian: Egyptian with Greek influences and inspirations.

Identification

Can we determine which Ptolemaic king this statue portrays? Despite the heavy damage to the face, it can be established that the portrait features were individualised. Noteworthy is how corpulent the head is, in stark contrast to the athletic body, as if the head and the body do not belong together. The face is full and fleshy, with a heavy protruding chin and round jowls on a taurine neck. The brows are marked as a single curve meeting horizontally over the bridge of the nose. The king's uneven eyes are comparatively small and have heavy lids; the upper semi-circular, the lower nearly straight. The uneven ears are set awkwardly high. His nose, though mostly damaged, appears to have been broad with flaring nostrils. The full lips are pursed into a stern smile. While no traces of pigments can be discerned, the viewer has to imagine that the face would have had the benefit of added painted details. The youthful, perhaps idealised smoothness of the physiognomy might thus be due to this lack of portrait detail.

On the basis of these physiognomic traits, the attribution to Ptolemy VIII is obvious. Various ancient sources inform us that the king was nicknamed Physkōn (Greek for blown up, puffed up or stuffed, in other words 'fatso'), a reference to his obesity.[9] The king's son, Ptolemy XI Soter II (*c.*143/2-81 BC), was also called by that derogatory nickname, but it is uncertain if he was ever portrayed as obese.[10] As Catharine Lorber points out, the cryptic portraiture issued on the authority of Ptolemy IX never adhered to the Physkōn-type.[11] His brother Ptolemy X Alexander (*c.*140/39-87 BC) was described as prone to obesity in lurid detail by Athenaios, quoting Poseidonios' *Histories*.[12] In other words, two or possibly three late-Ptolemaic kings could have been portrayed with full and fleshy facial features. Among the clay seal impressions from Ptolemaic Edfu, of which the Allard Pierson collection holds over three hundred specimens, there are dozens of Physkōn-type portraits that depict more than two individual kings (figs. 4a-d).[13] Lorber and I cannot attribute the seal impression that resembles the statue the most (fig. 4d) to a particular king with certainty on the basis of numismatic portraiture, which is the only reasonably sure means of identification. Personally, I do lean towards Ptolemy VIII, but there is insufficient evidence to support that intuition.

---

9 Polybios *Historiai,* 28.12; Strabo *Geographia,* 17.1; Josephos *Antiquitates Judaicae,* 12.228, 13.267; Athenaios *Deipnosophistai,* 12.73.

10 Jacoby 1930, *FGrH* nr. 252 (Capitoline Chronicle), col. 1, ll. 4–7 and 33–34; Eusebios *Chronicon,* 1.171.

11 Lorber (forthcoming).

12 Athenaios *Deipnosophistai,* 12.73.

13 Spier et al. 2018, no. 136; Lorber (forthcoming), figs. 36, 90, 94, 156.

Fig. 4 Four Physkōn-type glyptic portraits: (a) attributed to Ptolemy VIII; (b) attributed to Ptolemy X; (c) unidentified; and (d) perhaps Ptolemy VIII (?). Clay seal impressions; Edfu, Egypt; late Hellenistic, *c.*185-125 BC; APM08177-025, APM08196, APM08081 and APM08278. Images Allard Pierson, University of Amsterdam.

Conclusion

The fascinating statue of the Ptolemaic king in pharaonic guise cannot be attributed to Ptolemy VIII with certainty. Its sculptural style should be understood as an expression of Hellenistic Egyptian art, not so much because of its dating but more importantly because of its blend of old and new characteristics from both Greek and Egyptian cultural traditions. The Allard Pierson has every reason to be proud of this near-complete sculpture that does indeed best belong in its Hellenistic gallery.

Bibliography

Bissing, F.W. von, 1914, *Denkmäler ägyptischer Skulptur*, Munich.

Haarlem, W.M. van (ed.), 1986, *Corpus antiquitatum Aegyptiacarum Allard Pierson Museum, Amsterdam, Volume I, Selection from the Collection*, Mainz.

Iversen, E., 1975, *Canon and Proportions in Egyptian Art*, 2nd ed. with Y. Shibata, Warminster.

Jacoby, F. (ed.), 1930, *Die Fragmente der griechischen Historiker* [*FGrH*], II: Zeitgeschichte D: Kommentar zu Nr. 106-261, Berlin.

Lorber, C.C., (forthcoming), Coins and Sealings: The Portraiture of Ptolemy VI-XII, in Oppen de Ruiter, B.F. van, Wallenfels, R., (eds.), *Hellenistic Sealings & Archives Proceedings of The Edfu Connection, an International Conference, 23-24 January 2018, Allard Pierson Museum, Amsterdam, Studies in Classical Archaeology* 10, Turnhout.

Lunsingh Scheurleer, R.A., 1992, *Egypte, geschenk van de Nijl*, Steenwijk.

Lunsingh Scheurleer, R.A., Haarlem, W.M. van, 1986, *Gids voor de afdeling Egypte, Allard Pierson Museum Amsterdam*, Amsterdam.

Robins, G., 1994, *Proportion and Style in Ancient Egyptian Art*, London.

Stanwick, P.E., 2003, *Portraits of the Ptolemies: Greek Kings as Egyptian Pharaohs*, Austin.

Spier, J., Potts, T., Cole, S.E. (eds.), 2018, *Beyond the Nile: Egypt and the Classical World*, Los Angeles.

About the author

Dr Branko F. van Oppen de Ruiter is the Richard E. Perry Curator of Greek and Roman art of the Tampa Museum of Art, Florida. He is an ancient historian (CUNY GSUC PhD '07) with over a decade of wide-ranging teaching experience and specialises in Ptolemaic portraiture and royal ideology. Van Oppen has published on early Hellenistic queenship, clay seal impressions from Ptolemaic Edfu, animals in ancient material culture, and Romano-Egyptian mummy portraits, among other subjects. He was visiting researcher and guest curator at the Allard Pierson Museum from 2014 to 2018.

Re-excavating Gheyta's Roman-period cemetery

Some preliminary results on the recontextualisation of excavated artefacts

Ben van den Bercken

Introduction

In 2013 the Allard Pierson organised *The Petrie Perspective*, a project linked to the larger international project *Artefacts of Excavation: British Excavations in Egypt 1880-1980*, coordinated by University College London and Oxford University.[1] For the duration of the *Petrie Perspective* project, Willem van Haarlem worked on retracing 'Petrie objects' in the Allard Pierson to their moment of excavation. His work provided information on the historiography of objects excavated by the Egypt Exploration Fund (EEF), Egyptian Research Account (ERA) and British School of Archaeology in Egypt (BSAE).

This short contribution aims to start a recontextualisation of the 'artefacts of excavation' that Van Haarlem identified, as well as trace other objects from the same site. The site concerned in this contribution is the Roman cemetery of Gheyta in the eastern Nile Delta, which was excavated by the BSAE and ERA in 1905. As a tribute to and continuation of the work initiated by Willem van Haarlem this seemed a suitable contribution to this publication.

Recontextualising excavated artefacts

The results of the *Artefacts of Excavation* project clearly illustrated the migratory life of artefacts from British excavations in Egypt from 1880 to 1980, even after their initial distribution by the EEF, ERA and BSAE.[2] The results underlined the importance of documentation, as the objects might lose their original context at any next step in their historiography. Thanks to the project more detailed information about specific objects

1 See http://egyptartefacts.griffith.ox.ac.uk/.

2 See the below example of the Gheyta objects that went to Von Bissing.

in: Bercken, B.J.L. van den, 2021. *Egyptian Delta archaeology. Short studies in honour of Willem van Haarlem*, Leiden: Sidestone Press, pp. 121-130.

(re-)surfaced. A next step is to try and reconnect specific artefacts to the places where they were excavated and to virtually reunite them with the rest of the excavation material.[3]

The Egyptian collection of the Allard Pierson originated largely from the collection of the former Museum Scheurleer in The Hague. The banker Constant Willem Lunsingh Scheurleer (1881-1941) subscribed to the BSAE and EEF excavations and received several shipments between 1921 and 1927.[4] His collection also contained objects that Scheurleer acquired from Friedrich Wilhelm Freiherr von Bissing (1873-1956), who in his turn acquired them from the BSAE, ERA and EEF between 1902 and 1912. This latter group included objects from the BSAE and ERA excavation at Gheyta.

Gheyta/Tell Yehud

The cemetery at Gheyta (also Ghita) was excavated by the Revd John Garrow Duncan in the winter of 1905, while Petrie and other members of the team worked at Tell Yehudiya.[5] Duncan and his team operated from the nearby city of Bilbeis and excavated the Gheyta cemetery that was located near the ruins of Tell Yehud, a little east of the Ismailiyeh Canal. In four weeks' time they excavated an unknown number of graves on five different locations at the cemetery. These graves were dated from the first to the fourth century AD, based on the finds and grave types. The location of the cemetery has since become uncertain, as agricultural activity in the area has expanded even further.[6]

One is tempted to see the uncultivated area without construction south-west of Ezbet Abd el-Malak Saad as the site, fitting with Duncan's description that the ruins were already surrounded by agricultural lands. On the other hand, this location does not fit the description of 'about six miles from Belbeys'.[7] It is possible that the cemetery is now beneath the agricultural fields. Petrie did not spend much time on discussing Duncan's results in his introduction of the 1906 publication of his team's work. He merely states that 'the cemetery at Gheyta has shown how Syrian influence was coming into Egypt in the later centuries of Roman occupation.'[8] Duncan's interpretation of the name Gheyta as related to the Rhaetians, a people with a Levantine connection,[9] and the alabaster boxes for ointment[10] were used as arguments.

Reconstruction of Grave 71

Duncan and his team excavated a number of graves of different types.[11] Most of these had been plundered, which resulted in damage to the human remains and removal of grave goods which were often located near the head of the deceased.[12] Grave 71 was found intact. It belonged to the first type described by Duncan: a hole 'cut in the hard black soil to a depth of 7 or 8 feet.' On the bottom of the hole was 'a narrow slit wide enough to admit the body on its back, the rest of the width of the excavated hole being used as ledges to

3 E.g. the work of Franzmeier 2017, 3.
4 Van Haarlem 2016a, 9-10 and Van Haarlem 2016b.
5 Petrie 1906, I.
6 Duncan refers to this process already, Petrie 1906, 55.
7 Petrie 1906, 55.
8 Petrie 1906, 2-3.
9 Tóth 2008, 214-215.
10 Petrie 1906, 58.
11 Petrie 1906, 55-57.
12 Petrie 1906, 61.

Description	Material	Duncan No.	Current location	Inventory number
amphora	pottery	3	unknown	?
amphora	pottery	4	unknown	?
ointment box/jar/vase	alabaster	25	Manchester	3389
ointment box/jar/vase	alabaster	27	Manchester	3384
ointment box/jar/vase	alabaster	30	unknown	?
ointment box/jar/vase	alabaster	31	Manchester	3388
ointment box/jar/vase	alabaster	none	unknown	?
scarab	glazed steatite	59	Manchester	3420
scarab	glazed steatite	60	Manchester	3416
scarab	glazed steatite	61	Manchester	3417
scarab	glazed steatite	62	Manchester	3422
scarab	glazed steatite	63	Manchester	3419
scarab	dark stone	64	Manchester	3414
scarab	glazed steatite	65	Manchester	3421
scarab	glazed steatite	66	Manchester	3423
scarab	glazed steatite	67	Manchester	3413
scarab	glazed steatite	68	Manchester	3415
scarab	glazed steatite	69	Manchester	3418
spoon	bronze	91	Manchester	3387.a-d
spoon	bronze	92	Manchester	3387.a-d
cup	ivory	146	unknown	?
cup	ivory	147	unknown	?
cup	ivory	150	unknown	?
cup	ivory	154	unknown	?
pin	ivory?	158	unknown	?
ivory beads (bracelet)	ivory	161	Manchester?	3370.c?
fragments?	ivory?	163	unknown	?
bracelet(?) of beads	onyx	165	Manchester	3371
bead(s)	crystal(?)	170	Manchester	3371
rings (6x)	bronze	?	Edinburgh	A.1906.443.64; 64A; 64B; 64C; 64D; 66
shell for grinding kohl	shell	?	unknown	?
cylinder with 2 eyes	silver	none	Amsterdam	APM07026
cylinder with 2 eyes	silver	none	Manchester	3385
cylinder with 2 eyes	silver	none	Manchester	3386.a
cylinder with 2 eyes	silver	none	Manchester	3386.b
string of rough beads	limestone, carnelian, quartz	unknown	Manchester	3372

Fig. 1 Table of the finds from Gheyta Grave 71 that were traced in museum collections. The whereabouts of several objects are still unknown. Some may not have been preserved, for example the ivory cups, which were in a poor state of preservation when found by Duncan. In the table 'Manchester' refers to the Manchester Museum, 'Amsterdam' to the Allard Pierson and 'Edinburgh' to the National Museums Scotland.

support the stone slabs or bricks placed over the corpse after burial.'[13] Duncan does not explicitly specify, but interprets the buried person as a female.[14] Finds from the grave included ivory cups, alabaster boxes for ointment, bronze spoons, beads, a cosmetic shell, pharaonic scarabs, silver cylinder pendants and, near the surface of the grave's filling, two inscribed amphora fragments. These finds were dispersed over several museums and the Von Bissing collection in 1905-1906, and some have changed hands since. Untill now, only several objects kept at the Manchester Museum and one object from the Allard Pierson were attributed to Grave 71. With the help of the EEF/ERA/BSAE distribution lists, online museum databases and the valuable help of museum curators a large part of the objects mentioned by Duncan as having come from Grave 71 has now been traced (fig. 1).[15] This is a first step in the recontextualisation process.

Some notes on artefacts from Gheyta Grave 71

Analysis of the finds from Grave 71 and other graves is under way. Some of the main questions are how local the grave goods were and whether Duncan's dating of the graves can be refined on the basis of parallels from elsewhere. Some of the grave goods are particularly interesting.

During excavation nine 'alabaster boxes for ointment' were found. Of these cosmetic boxes or *pyxides*, five were found in Grave 71 (fig. 1). This could be an indication of the relative wealth or preferences of its occupant, but also of the bad state of preservation of other graves at the site (fig. 2). Presently, no exact parallels for these boxes are known from other Roman period cemeteries in the Delta.[16] Alabaster ointment jars of various types are well known in pharaonic Egypt;[17] in the Byzantine period Alexandrian workshops produced ivory *pyxides* of great quality.[18] The shape and decoration patterns of the Gheyta boxes recall earlier pottery *pyxides* from the Late Helladic (fourteenth-thirteenth century BC).[19] No Egyptian parallels for this type of box have been found yet. Were the Gheyta boxes unique and perhaps made locally? Or are they products of 'Syrian influence', as Petrie and Duncan stated? Research into these questions is ongoing.

That the person buried in Grave 71 had a relation with objects from the past is clear from the series of pharaonic scarabs that was found near the right wrist. These date from the 13th to the 19th dynasty and must have been collected and made into a contemporary bracelet.[20] Although mentioned in one sentence by Duncan, this is in fact an interesting and yet little-investigated phenomenon, and a fresh dimension to the

13 Petrie 1906, 55.

14 Petrie 1906, 61-62.

15 I would especially like to thank Campbell Price (Manchester Museum), Daniel Potter (National Museums Scotland), Tony Jonges and Geralda Jurriaans-Helle (both Allard Pierson) for their help in tracing the objects. Manchester Museum accession number 3414 was published in Boschloos 2012, 8 and 15.

16 E.g. at Minshat Abu Omar (Kroeper 1988, 12); Quesna (Rowland 2008, 70); Kafr Hassan Dawood (Lovell 1997, 36-37); Tell el-Maskhuta (Holladay 1982, 37-43); and Tell Belim (Spencer 2002, 40-42).

17 E.g. Von Bissing 1904, Plate IX.

18 Rodziewicz, 2003, 47-70.

19 Fourteenth-thirteenth century BC, e.g. Metropolitan Museum of Art (accession numbers 74.51.772 and 74.51.767) and British Museum (e.g. accession number 1897,0401.1280). The shape also resembles New Kingdom kohl jars (e.g. Rijksmuseum van Oudheden, Leiden inventory number AAL 100).

20 These scarabs are now in the Manchester Museum, accession numbers 3413-3423.

Fig. 2 One of the alabaster boxes from Grave 71. Image Manchester Museum, University of Manchester, accession number 3384.

Artefacts of Excavation.[21] Some of the scarabs were already two thousand years old at that time. The phenomenon of reuse of scarabs has been addressed by Othmar Keel, who differentiates between *Erbstücke* and *Findlinge*.[22] The difference in dates of the scarabs from Grave 71 seems to point to (accidental) collecting and reuse, which does not mean that the ensemble might not have functioned as an heirloom at any stage between the 19th dynasty and Roman period.[23] Duncan refers to other graves at Gheyta, where older scarabs were exclusively found in graves of women and children. Comparison might provide further insights.

In the collection of the Allard Pierson Van Haarlem identified three Gheyta objects: a gold and glass earring (APM07023), a cylindrical silver pendant (APM07026) and a small glass bottle (APM07697). Only the cylindrical pendant came from Grave 71; it originally belonged to a set of four (fig. 3). The exact find location in the grave has not been recorded, but these four elements probably were parts of one piece of jewellery, although it cannot be excluded that they functioned as individual pendants, possibly with small stones set into them. Similar silver and gold links are known from pendants, necklaces and bracelets, often as ends.[24] Several beads, including a set of onyx interpreted

21 Research on reuse in ancient Egypt often focuses on coffins, tombs and monuments, where reuse involves practical, economic and political motivations, e.g. Arbuckle MacLeod/Cooney 2019, Creasman 2013 and Brand 2010. The (re-)use of non-monumental objects from earlier times remains an interesting field of research to be developed further.

22 Keel 1995, 262-263.

23 For references to reused scarabs in Roman burials, see Keel 1995, 263.

24 For parallels, see Marshall 1911, nos. 2273, 2736, 2736*, 2737, 2813, 2814 and 2964. Several date from the second-third centuries AD.

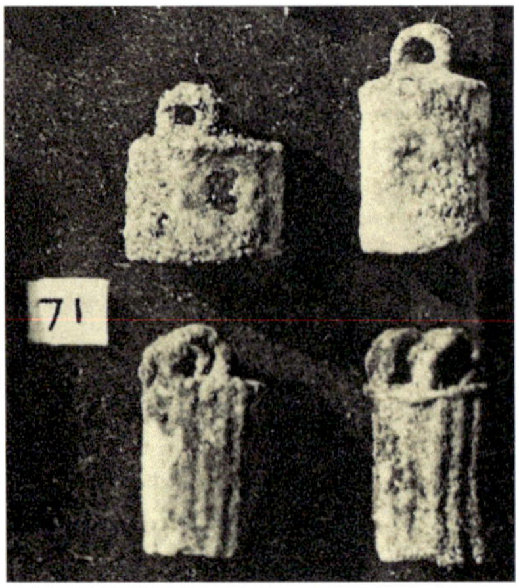

Fig. 3 The four silver pendants from Grave 71 after excavation. After Petrie 1906, Plate XL.

Fig. 4 Onyx and crystal beads necklace from Grave 71. Image Manchester Museum, University of Manchester, accession number 3371.

by Duncan as a bracelet (fig. 4) and a set of ivory beads, were found in Grave 71. Possibly one of these sets and the badly preserved silver pendants were once parts of the same piece of jewellery.

Concluding

This contribution is but a small next step in mapping, describing and analysing the Roman-period cemetery at Gheyta. Research into the Gheyta objects in the Allard Pierson and elsewhere is being continued and will contribute to a corpus of grave goods that shows interesting local variations in burial practices and objects. In the end it will help us to better understand the people of these sites outside the regional and national centres of Roman Egypt.

Bibliography

Arbuckle MacLeod, C., Cooney, K., 2019, The layered life of JE26204: the construction and reuse of the coffins of Henuttawy, *Journal of Egyptian Archaeology* 105 (2), 285-296.

Bissing, F. von, 1904, *Catalogue Général des Antiquités Égyptiennes du Musée du Caire. Steingefässe*, Vienne.

Boschloos, V., 2012, Late Bronze Age cornelian and red jasper scarabs with cross designs: Egyptian, Levantine or Minoan? *Journal of Ancient Egyptian Interconnections* 4 (2), 5-16.

Brand, P., 2010, Reuse and restoration, in Wendrich, W. (ed.), 2010, *UCLA Encyclopedia of Egyptology*, 1-15, via https://escholarship.org/uc/item/2vp6065d (accessed November 2020).

Creasman, P., 2013, Ship timber and the reuse of wood in ancient Egypt, *Journal of Egyptian History* 6 (2), 152-176.

Petrie, W.M.F., 1906, *Hyksos and Israelite Cities*, London.

Franzmeier, H., 2017, *Die Gräberfelder von Sedment im Neuen Reich. Materielle und kulturelle Variation im Bestattungswesen des ägyptischen Neuen Reiches*, Leiden/Boston.

Haarlem, W. van, 2016a, Petrie en het Allard Pierson Museum, *Allard Pierson Mededelingen* 111/112, 9-15.

Haarlem, W. van, 2016b, *Eindrapport project 'Petrie Perspectief'* (unpublished, but shorter version published at https://egyptartefacts.griffith.ox.ac.uk/?q=objects-petrie-excavations-allard-pierson-museum-results-petrie-perspective-project, accessed November 2020).

Holladay, J., 1982, *Cities of the Delta, part III: Tell el-Maskhuta. Preliminary report on the Wadi Tumilat Project 1978-1979*, Malibu.

Keel, O., 1995, *Corpus der Stempelsiegel-Amulette aus Palästina/Israel. Von den Anfängen bis zur Perserzeit. Einleitung. Orbis Biblicus et Orientalis, Series Archaeologica* 10. Göttingen.

Kroeper, K., 1988, The excavations of the Munich East-Delta Expedition in Minshat in Abu Omar, in Van den Brink, E.C.M. (ed.), *The archaeology of the Nile Delta, Egypt: problems and priorities. Proceedings of the seminar held in Cairo, 19-22 October 1986, on the occasion of the fifteenth anniversary of the Netherlands Institute of Archaeology and Arabic Studies in Cairo*, Amsterdam, 11-46.

Lovell, N., 1997, The 1995 excavations of the cemetery at Kafr Hassan Daoud, Wadi Tumilat, *Journal of the Society for the Study of Egyptian Antiquities* 27, 34-41.

Marshall, F., 1911, *Catalogue of the jewellery, Greek, Etruscan and Roman in the departments of antiquities, British Museum*, London.
Rodziewicz, E., 2003, On Alexandrian school of ivory carvings in late antiquity, *Société Archéologique d'Alexandrie Bulletin* 47, 47-70.
Rowland, J., 2008, The Ptolemaic-Roman cemetery at the Quesna Archaeological Area, *Journal of Egyptian Archaeology* 94, 69-93.
Spencer, J., 2002, The exploration of Tell Belim, 1999-2002, *Journal of Egyptian Archaeology* 88, 37-51.
Stevenson, A., 2013, Artefacts of excavation. The British collection and distribution of Egyptian finds to museums 1880-1915, *Journal of the History of Collections* 26 (1), 89-102.
Tóth, A., 2008, The origin of the Rhaetians, *Anthropos* 103:1, 210-216.

About the author

Ben van den Bercken is an archaeologist and junior curator of Egyptian antiquities at the Allard Pierson, University of Amsterdam. Formerly, he was assistant curator of Engraved Gems at the National Museum of Antiquities, Leiden. His work on the Leiden collection of engraved gems includes contributions to the collection's history and studies of Egyptian scarabs and Egyptian cylinder seals. He worked at excavations in Alexandria, Egypt. Presently, he is working on the history of the Egyptian collection of the Allard Pierson and a project on mummy portraits.